Gorbals Boy
at Oxford

RALPH GLASSER

Chatto & Windus

LONDON

Published in 1988 by
Chatto & Windus Ltd
30 Bedford Square
London WC1B 3RP

British Library Cataloguing in Publication Data
Glasser, Ralph
Gorbals Boy at Oxford.
1. Glasser, Ralph   2. Great Britain
– Biography
I. Title
941.082'092'4   CT788.G5/

ISBN 0-7011-3185-3

Photoset in Linotron Ehrhardt by
Rowland Phototypesetting Ltd
Bury St Edmunds, Suffolk
Printed in Great Britain by
Redwood Burn Ltd
Trowbridge, Wiltshire

To Jacqueline, my Egĕria

Contents

Goodbye Gorbals

Talking to John Betjeman in his room at Blenheim Palace, I happened to mention that I had come up to Oxford from the Gorbals. Part of the palace was in use by departments of the British Council, still in wartime evacuation quarters. He was standing before one of the huge panels of biscuit-coloured plywood covering the walls of the little salon which, like most of the rooms put to office use, still carried this protection for delicate surfaces beneath. He had been chalking on it a complicated notation of change-ringing. Betjeman had a job at the Council as Administrator of the Arts and Science Division, to which he had come from being Press Attaché at the Embassy in Dublin. His present duties could not have been burdensome; to judge from the vast arrangement of chalk marks he had drawn on the board, he had spent most of the morning at it. He turned, the loose lower lip, drawn to the left as always, sagging further, and searched my face, plainly wondering what to say, which was unusual for him. Then, resuming the habitual mandarin drawl, half-eager, half blasé, said, 'You *must* tell me how the place struck you – I suppose "struck" is the word! Dear boy, did the architecture transform you?'

In pre-war days, for a Gorbals man to come up to Oxford was as unthinkable as to meet a raw bushman in a St James's club – something for which there were no stock responses. In any case, for a member of the boss class, someone from the Gorbals *was* in effect a bushman, the Gorbals itself as distant, as unknowable, as the Kalahari Desert. Betjeman, plainly unable to fit the phenomenon into any context he understood, had picked on a theme in which he did feel comfortable. Externals were his forte.

In one sense, his instinct was accurate, to probe for the first, aesthetic, impact of the place. At the time of this conversation at Blenheim, a piquant convergence in itself, as he was quick to point out, my first arrival on my bike, though some six years behind me, was still fresh, not yet in perspective. *That* would take many years. I tried to re-create it for him, as I then understood it.

He was a good listener when he cared to suppress the urge to interject a bright sixth-form quip whenever one paused for breath. He stepped away from the wallboard, baggy beige clothes hanging sack-like, and sat down at his desk, swinging round to face me in the armchair at his side, forgetting to relinquish the chalk. Possessed as when he had stood with me contemplating the poetry of Keble, he raptly traced my words on some inner palimpsest of his own.

Despite what seemed arrogant posturing, and certainly a core of toughness, he had a timid, gentle streak, carefully protected. When I had finished he said, the sideways smile returning, 'You *must* write about it one day. There's so much more to that journey isn't there – like a second birth?'

I wheeled the bike out of our flat on the third, top floor of the Gorbals tenement, and leaned it against the iron stairhead railing. I turned and pulled the door shut, and was about to put the key in the lock when something made me step back and contemplate the battered old doorway, an eerie command to etch the image on my mind, its meaning for me through the years. It seemed that I saw it for the first time, the door hanging crooked in its frame, its dark brown paint chipped and scratched and flaked away by time and damp, yet still possessing a certain dignity, the slender flutings enclosing the six panels, the fine rings in relief on the brass knob-plate, the ringed boss on the brass knob itself, the keyhole plate scrolled at the top and waisted like a violin; all battered and begrimed, never touched with Brasso since that day, long ago, when mother died.

The finality of the moment, unbelievable, held me fast. Surely nothing was ever finished? One day another word, another deed, would be added to the account to change the judgment? Standing here on the cold stone landing, part of me fiercely wanted to write 'finis' under it all. Another voice told me I *must* not, could not. That was not for human hand to do.

'Vengeance is mine, I will repay . . .'

Indeed the place was already receding from me. I would carry the bike down the winding stone stairs and ride away, further than I had ever travelled, to take up the scholarship. For this journey there was no name, no measure. I thought of the times when, as a child, staring through the black window panes at night, I soared far away among the stars. This time the journey would be real. I would not return. I might stand here again physically, but I would never feel the spiritual breath of this place, palpably on my face, as I did now.

I checked that the straps closing the shiny black saddlebag of oiled canvas were buckled fast; and those securing the oilskin cape across it. The bag was packed tight with three changes of underclothes, two khaki shirts, socks, trousers – I wore khaki shorts for the journey – and a thick woollen jersey with sleeves; nearly all from the army surplus stores. Food was in the outer pouches; a small loaf of black bread, three hard-boiled eggs, a slab of cheese, a bag of raisins, milk in a medicine bottle, tobacco tins containing tea, sugar, salt, matches, and Metafuel for the primus stove clamped under the cross bar. I could carry no more. A parcel containing a few other clothes, all I could afford in the list sent by the college, with the only books I possessed – *Chambers's Dictionary*, Hegel's *Logic*, Fisher's *History of Europe*, the whole bought with the loan from Aunt Rachel – I had sent ahead by rail.

When Meyer the boxer joined the army, to escape the debt collectors' retribution, after he had knocked them out for beating up poor Mr Fredericks in the street, his father sold me his bike, fully equipped, for two pounds, which I was still paying off at a shilling a month; it had the new derailleur gear change, dropped handlebars, and the luxury of dynamo lighting in place of the conventional acetylene gas lamp. I was in good training, and looking forward to the test of doing a hundred miles a day. I would stay at Cyclists' Touring Club bed-and-breakfast houses for ninepence a night.

Father had left for work at seven. We had parted in an atmosphere of apocalyptic phlegm, overlaying an uneasy, hesitant, stilted kindliness. The hooded figure of the wounded past stood beside us counselling forbearance, generosity if not forgiveness, at this close of an epoch. Years later I would see that the old epoch had begun to die long before, on the day I found he had pawned my suit. Oh that suit!

That parting in the cold grey kitchen, the imprisoned passion, the forlorn longing to recreate love and gentleness, still lacerates the spirit. Tumult roared within – the desire to erase the past, pity for him, remorse at leaving him, eagerness to take my chance away from him, the tingle of adventure, voices of doubt, foreboding. If only I could find the calm, the lucidity, to

———

close the distance between us, spread out before him all that I felt about the present and the past and the future, smooth away all anger, all hurt, make him see that I had no choice but to go. I saw the disappointment in him, the defeat. I saw that he longed to understand and sympathise, to reach out to me, but that he could come only a fragment of the way. He knew why I was stricken dumb, but could not help me utter the truths that clamoured to be set free, perhaps because he too could not open his heart. We both had too much to say, and no words fitted.

I knew that for him the parting was cataclysmic. He did not see my going to Oxford as Bernard's father did, as a romantic, heroic quest, but prosaically as doing something 'to better myself'. In attempted stoicism – his only reply to Fate over the years – he did try to accept that I must follow my star, as he and others of his generation had done long ago when they had left *der heim* to seek fulfilment in the melting pot of another culture. For me, as it had been for him, 'it was written' – *es shtayt geshreeben* – it had to be. He could not have failed to see in my going a re-enactment, in reverse, of that day when as a young man he had set out to meet the unknown. He divined, I think more clearly than I did, that I too would journey to a world light years distant from these my roots, as he had done from his.

In the cold kitchen, in the grey morning light, as he stood ready to go to work, we faced each other, at the end, in silence. As always he was neatly dressed, navy blue overcoat, blue serge suit, white collarless shirt and grey woollen muffler, grey felt hat with black silk band. His tools were in a small Gladstone bag on the cracked oilcloth table cover. He looked deep into my eyes and then at the floor; would the Almighty send a sign to stop me going? At last he held out his hand and gripped mine hard: '*Gey gesunterheyt*' (Go in health). He picked up the bag, blue-grey eyes looking at nothing, turned, squaring his shoulders, and strode out.

Downstairs, I wheeled the bike over the broken flagstones in the close, absently avoiding the little heaps of putrescent rubbish and rat droppings. Out on the pavement I heaved it round to set it in the gutter pointing south, the near pedal propped on the pavement edge, and sat on the saddle, one foot on the raised pedal and pressed into the toe-clip ready to move off.

The coalman stood on his cart at the far end of the street, his powerful bass booming out 'Caw-aw-aw-aw-awl!'; the organ-grinder and the tin-

4

whistle man kept their judicious distances behind him, hoping for the odd penny wrapped in newspaper to come down from a window. Women hurried past – dodging with raised skirt-hems the litter of horse droppings, rotting fish heads and vegetable matter, vomit – on their way to shops, the Steamy, the pawnshop, or to deliver washing 'taken in'. A few men slouched past aimlessly to congregate at the corners; it was too early for pubs. Some would make their way, later, to the offices of the *Evening Citizen* whose 'Situations Vacant' page would be displayed, for those who could not afford to buy the paper, in a wire-fronted case outside the back entrance in St Vincent Place across the Clyde; but that would not be till noon.

I sat and stared; something was hidden that I must uncover and take with me; some furtive spirit of that life, a talisman, a reference point from which to take my bearings wherever I went. It was there; of that I was certain. But it hid from me.

I dug my foot on the raised pedal and pushed away, head down, impatient now to be away on the open road and there, in the hypnotic rhythm of pedalling, lose myself in thoughts of what awaited at the other end.

In the afternoon, ten miles after the long climb up to Beattock Summit, two things happened, almost at the same moment, to force me off the bike; either, by itself, would have been enough. I got 'the knock', the sudden draining of energy from the legs; and the chain jumped off the gear train. The cure for the knock was food; for the chain, a spike to dig out a stone that must have lodged in a link. I looked about for shelter. I needed to put the stove, myself too, behind a windbreak. I must be quick; twilight was near, and I had twenty-five miles to cover to reach the bed-and-breakfast house. On these bleak approaches to the bald Cheviot hills, a keen south-west wind swept across the road; and there was not a tree or hedgerow or wall in sight. I spotted a layby a few hundred yards further on, littered with concrete blocks and pieces of timber. Stiff-legged, I wheeled the bike towards it, the jumped chain rattling angrily against the rear fork. I longed for a mug of scalding tea, and a doorstep of bread and cheese. Luckily I had brought water from my last stop in a screwtop container – another ex-army item – for there was not a burn, or for that matter a house, anywhere in sight. In this deserted land near the border, burns were hard to find.

I leaned the bike against a stack of timber, quickly assembled the primus and, in the lee of some concrete blocks, got it alight despite the wind, and put the billy can on to boil; then upended the bike and stood it on saddle and handlebars to deal with the chain. Another purchase from the army surplus stores was a clasp knife fitted with a long spike, presumably an all-purpose implement for life in the trenches; with it I gouged the stone out of the chain and re-threaded it into position in the gear train.

Absorbed, I had been dimly aware of the approaching rumble of a heavy vehicle. Hands oily from the chain, I stepped to the raised bank at the rear of the layby to rub my hands clean on the grass, my back to the road; there was a grating of brakes, the slam of a door and crack-crack of steel-shod boots on the road and a shout: 'Fuckin' hell! Whi' are *yew* doin' here?'

Meyer Melek shone in glory. There was something more than the ruddiness of the outdoor life, an added stature, a calm, an acceptance of power, and of acclaim. Meyer was lightweight champion of the Command. On his sleeve were corporal's stripes and the badge of P.T. instructor. About a dozen soldiers now clattered down on to the road from the tarpaulin-covered rear of the truck and drew near to him, their faces aglow with hero-worship. Only later did I learn how men at arms forgave a man almost anything, even being a Jew, if he was a physical star. The more aggressive the sport the more open their hearts – to, supremely, the boxer.

Meyer was in the Engineers. He was returning with his squad from a last field exercise before an overseas posting; he thought it would be to Singapore. Seeing him wistfully contemplating the bike, I told him that when he got out of the army he could have it back; meanwhile I would look after it well. We dared not say what was in our minds; the Fates probably had other plans. In the army, he said, everyone pretended it was still a peacetime world; but no one felt sure of anything any more. What had happened to the old imperial certainty you learnt at school, that used to hold everything solid?

He worried about his father's ill-health, and whether he could keep the little workshop going if things got worse and his brothers were called up.

I had last seen him on the day the 'menodge men', sent to exact retribution for his interference – after he had stopped them beating up Mr Fredericks for being behind in his debt repayments – had given him their ultimatum. The next morning he had gone up to Maryhill Barracks to escape them. Years later, that would strike me as another of the Fates' ironic tricks, for in a sense he had fled the lesser doom; the menodge men had threatened to do no more than finish his boxing career by damaging his hands – if, that is, he refused to join them. But he would not survive building the death railway for the Japanese. This was the last time I saw him.

In the gathering twilight, on the lonely, anonymous road that was taking us God alone knew where, on tangents far from the world we knew, we shook hands in silent tribute to the felicity of this ordained meeting, acknowledging the fears and doubts that dwarfed us.

'The glass is falling hour by hour,
The glass will fall for ever . . .'

The others clambered raucously into the truck. Meyer stepped up into the cab next to the driver, and the heavy vehicle rumbled away on the empty road, heading south too. I watched its lights draw away, and disappear, then went back into the layby and gulped some tea and packed up; I mounted and rode hard after it, head down over the handlebars, trying to think of nothing.

Seeing him departing into the shadowy future, a fellow-exile, loneliness was diluted. We were voyagers together. The ambiguities of this encounter were those of life itself; they would persist, tantalisingly, in all I did, wherever I went. Meyer had never been as close to me as Bernard – Communist firebrand, returned disillusioned from the Spanish War – at least not in the same confiding, questing fashion. Meyer, like Alec who worked opposite me in the factory, did not examine life; he lived it. His sympathy and warmth, a gentleness that went hand in hand with his strength, were given sparingly, tokens of trust, regard, duty. Not overtly religious, his morality was fixed in the old rock of Moses, unquestioned. He was a man of simple, unambiguous values, who acted surely, unwaveringly, without reflection, come what may. Long ago in childhood these qualities must have drawn me to him, a natural alliance of sympathy, valued without thought. Many years later I would understand that his was the sureness I had always wanted to possess. Now, as he departed, I knew that I would carry his spiritual presence with me always, a steady point of light in moments of doubt. A premonition may have told me to mark that moment in my memory; I would honour him in my heart always.

Four days later, at about ten in the morning, I rode into Oxford in the middle of a cloudburst, the rain sheeting down in great wet curtains such as I would not see until, many years later in Pakistan, the monsoon rains fell down in masses from the sky. I had decided to spend the night at a Cyclists' Touring Club house a few miles short of Oxford, so that my first sight of the place would be in daylight. Coming in from the north, the Banbury Road was awash up to kerb height, my wheels swishing through the rushing brown waters. The screens of trees and shrubbery guarding the tall Victorian houses glistened wetly in brilliant greens and reddish browns, thin streams of water tumbling from leaf to leaf like myriad little waterfalls. The deluge must have driven every living soul indoors, leaving a perspective of broad, cambered road, ample pavements interrupted by wide driveways flanked by massive wooden gateposts topped with romantic wrought iron fantasies, a tree-sheltered world, settled, comfortable, ordered; an Elysian contrast with the world I had left behind. To the people in these tall, protected houses, I saw that my world would be not only unknown; it would be incredible. That was a shock to begin with.

The rain ceased and the grey skies lifted, and soon, instead of riding crouched within the sweating rain-cape, I sat up and flung the cape back and rode slowly, hands resting on the handlebars in the high position, and looked round at ease. In the Mitchell Library I had studied photographs of Oxford; but now, nearing the centre, a vision rose up out of the earth more powerful than any picture. In feeling totally foreign to the comfortable North Oxford of evergreens and tall brick houses, here was a world of citadels and power, with echoes of lawless times, the iron tread of men-at-arms, the embattled order of the church. So astounding was it, so awesome and yet so magnetic, that I forgot my immediate purpose, to present myself at the college, and rode on through the old precincts, winding through alleys and under blind college walls, beating the bounds of the grey monastic *mise en scène* again and again, tracing the map imprinted in memory. I knew that I was seeing it as I would never see it again, and that I must absorb this first impact in its completeness. Here was a world that flaunted mediaeval certainty, the caprice of secular riches and of clerical power, the tenacious retention of old categories, a secretive world of prejudices grimly maintained. Each turret, machicolation, mullion, buttress, each baronial portico, each fortress doorway that might easily have sheltered behind a portcullis, spoke of protected domains of flinty rule, of secret follies and public arrogance. This was not the blessedly illuminated world that Bernard's father dreamt I was joining, of simple savants dispensing gentleness and light and humanity, but a hard, jealous, defensive one.

Through half-closed eyes I saw grey-cowled figures, secure in grace, putting heretics to the torture or the stake.

Catching at the heart, however, there was also a delicate, fugitive beauty, a poetic spirit that this old jealous monasticism could neither contain nor banish, silver voices trapped in the stone.

At last, in Radcliffe Square, that seemed to enclose the innermost spirit of the place, I stood and contemplated the combination of lumpy ostentation, dignity, simplicity, baroque detachment and coldness. I heard a gravelly voice near me, incongruously formal, trembling with pathos. It came from a stocky man, military-looking, with bristling grey moustache, dressed in a bright blue blazer and pale trousers and a white shirt with an orange bow tie, and a boater with an orange ribbon. He punctuated his words by tapping the ground with a thick malacca stick. He was, I would later discover, known as the Major, an official Oxford City guide. Addressing a middle-aged couple, he had the air of making an important pronouncement. Catching my glance, he beckoned me over with a wave of the stick, to include me in what he had to say: 'Always remember this, my friends. Going into the gun room and ending your troubles is the easy way. But it is *wrong*. The Bible says so. Don't do it, I beg of you. Pass it on.' He raised the boater and stumped away.

I would hear of his sad fate about a year later.

I thought of this sad coming together here, in this fortress of past certainties, dwarfed by rich indifference and gothic chill. Inexplicably, that gruff military voice, with its shattering exposure of inner pain, recalled the drum-like voice of the Clincher crying out, too, for a warmer, kindlier world. The gun room? What world did that man come from? That apart, in this setting of arrogance, over-ripeness, wintry power, those words were frighteningly fitting.

Standing here, I felt more of an outsider than I had ever dreamed possible. Where among these blind strongholds would I find a weak point, a sympathetic wicket gate, to enter and find my rightful place?

9

The Citadel Takes Over

In retrospect, John Betjeman may have been right after all. 'Dear boy, did the architecture transform you?' may not have been as absurd a question as I had thought.

Of all the influences at work in those first days and months, the physical must have been the most potent; the arrogant baroque and neo-gothic and what they stood for, proclaiming certainty, permitting no challenge, seized me, gauche and impatient spirit that I was, and threw bridle and harness upon me. Here was order, fixity, unquestioning and unquestioned. How wonderful to feel such confidence!

In these comfortable, complacent bourgeois streets, still those of a tight little country town – where not a fish-head or boiled-out meat bone lay in the gutter, where even the poor areas of Jericho and Paradise Square were 'respectable' by Gorbals standards – black-gowned figures inhabited every perspective. Wherever you went, power and tradition were inescapable, brushing aside the pretended languor and indifference of the privileged denizens, those who truly belonged. For the vast majority of them, I assumed, the ethos was not totally new as it was to me, but was received essentially as a continuation of school, richer perhaps, more theatrical and stylised, but essentially of the same order, irksome sometimes but only in the sense that the complex minuet of a large settled family might be. That, I reflected, must be why Oxford did not fall upon them with anything like the shock of a completely alien culture, a new way of life and thinking invading the spirit, as it did on me. Oxford must be their recent past writ large, a pattern of thought and manners already absorbed, a drill-manual to be put on a shelf, no longer referred to except as an instinctive refuge in time of crisis. Many affected to reject it altogether, a pretence that at first deceived me, and I wondered at the paradox – that we should be going in opposite directions, *they* appearing to scorn the codes of this place while I strove to acquire them! Later I would see that they were not truly in rebellion; and that it was only because they stood so solidly – if unknowingly – upon the beliefs of this place that they were secure enough to put on a show of disdain. I had no such certainty. I trod the unknown at every step, fearful of stumbling. For me the drill manual was something to absorb as quickly as possible – the insecure ardour of the *arriviste*.

I went into the grey monastic quad of the Bodleian, the Old School quad, and read the legend in gold above each doorway, Scola Mathematica, Scola Physica – the sovereign estates of the mind laid out as on a chart, once again a picture of certainty, the ways made distinct and clear. I climbed the wooden staircase, short flights ascending within a square dusty shaft, beside a wide wooden balustrade of ducal proportions, each broad tread worn down in two concave patches – I saw the uninterrupted procession marching up and down in file over the generations. In a little musty room I signed the register of Bodleian readers. Being told that I was now a member for life, the moment took on apocalyptic significance, like that in the factory, on my last day there before leaving for Oxford, when I shut off the main power switch in a final gesture, and felt that an epoch had slid away for ever. Here, with the register before me, was my first true step into the citadel, a person fully recognised. Here in a different sense I could say, with father, '*es shtayt geshreeben!*' In the Gorbals I had had little sense of being a person in my own right – rather it was a fragile, secret identity, timidly guarded, whose signature was evanescent, written in the rain on the pavements on my way to the Mitchell Library, in the decaying rubbish carpeting the flagstones in close and pavement.

Here was a gentler contrast with my first impression of the citadel, when I had stood out there in Radcliffe Square beyond these grey walls, and the grandiose *mise en scène*, showy perpendicular and gross baroque, drying after the wild downpour, had glistened with the menace of old steel, and I had felt a shiver of fear contending with longing and hope. Here was my name inscribed for all time in the very heart of it! Its lances were raised; its sword points were lowered – provisionally.

It is hard to believe that I could have thought of the Bodleian in these momentous terms – perhaps I had given the Mitchell Library an equal sanctity? – and that I was callow enough to be shocked when others appeared to treat it with scant respect. There was Hamish, confirmed practical joker, who donned stage make-up and a false beard and, pretending serious research, persuaded a member of the Bodleian staff to bring him John Wilkes' *Essay on Woman* – a work so scandalous that it was on the restricted access list – and copied it out for *zamizdat* circulation among a select few:

> 'Awake my Fanny, leave all meaner things,
> This morn shall show what rapture swiving brings . . .'

I accepted a copy, on several sheets of smudged carbon, and for many weeks hid it in the lining of my trunk, expecting that at any moment, in some fateful fashion, the sin would proclaim itself.

In the smallest of day-to-day matters, there was a whole new alphabet to be learnt, the manners and controls of a totally different regime of living – you did not, for example, use certain Anglo-Saxon words with the unthinking freedom we did in the Gorbals. It seemed at first that every single response to life must always be muted, till I understood that the codes, though the form might be silken, could in Gladstonian fashion be ferocious: 'Suaviter in modo, fortiter in re.'

I realised, too, that I must not show surprise at the ways of this new world, for that made you vulnerable; I must quickly present myself in a new and permanently changed persona. That meant wearing a mask while I sloughed off the old skin – fearful always that the mask might slip. Sometimes, looking in the mirror, I could understand how Hoffman felt when his reflection was stolen – the 'I' that I had known was not here!

I had never, for instance, had a room of my own, where I could shut my door and read or write or dream, or have guests – that, too, a new experience – precisely as I chose. I could burn the light in my room at night as long as I liked with no fear of having to search for pennies for the meter. For the first few weeks this feeling of possessing sovereign territory was unnerving. I paced up and down restlessly, glorying in this new state, but at the same time feeling that I had lost whatever bearings I had ever had. With dismay, even shame, I regarded the bookshelves beside my writing table – a writing table all to myself! – empty except for my pitiful stock of three books, one of them a dictionary; I thought of other students' rooms with well-stocked shelves, ornaments, bric-a-brac, pieces of a well-found home life.

Pyjamas symbolised another dramatic change. I had never owned any; for years I had slept in my 'semmit', vernacular for undervest. When I first put on my newly-bought pyjamas I said to myself: What a waste of money – still, it is 'the done thing'! Similarly, following the guidance list thoughtfully sent me, I had bought a dressing-gown, an unbelievable luxury known only from films. What was it for, I wondered – after all, when you got out of bed you simply put on your clothes! Presumably you wore it when you went to have a bath or to the lavatory? In the Gorbals one used a chamber pot or, for 'Number twos', slipped on shirt and trousers and went out of the house to the shared lavatory on the stairhead. Slippers, too, were another enigmatic extravagance! As for baths, in the Gorbals the day of the domestic bathroom for the lower orders was not yet; you went to the public 'slipper baths' near the Steamy, the public wash-house, or made do with a hot shower after a swim; here there were baths of gentlemanly dimensions, long enough to lie in at full length, where you could soak for as long as you wished, whenever the caprice possessed you. Nearly everyone else here, amazingly, had a bath *every* day!

Nor could I get used to lying abed after five o'clock in the morning, my usual waking time in the busy season at the factory. For most of my first term I rose at that time and bathed and shaved and dressed, and read till breakfast time – until neighbours complained about the noise I made in the echoing ablutions, when I ran a bath or flushed the toilet and sometimes, forgetfully, strolled about whistling.

College life was in many ways burdensome, a teasing mixture of independent sovereignty and the constraints of community. One was surrounded by people with strange tastes and preferences, to adapt to or steer clear of; there were so many pitfalls to avoid, and always the nagging awareness that others seemed to navigate without any special care, but that my vigilance must never relax.

The greatest shock was the social discipline, ceremonial, tribal. The regularity of meals, for instance, was inexplicably irksome; in the Gorbals I ate – if there was food in the house – when I was hungry, and as often as not alone; here it was an undeviating ritual at long refectory tables and hard benches, that joined you to your neighbour in a formal compulsion of manner and speech, even in the passing of bread and salt. Above all, there was the burden of obligatory conversation – burden partly because I did not know the codes of what was acceptable, and because the talk seemed deliberately directionless yet mysteriously selective. Its purpose, slowly grasped – as Stevenson at the Institute of Experimental Psychology would put it – was to establish one's place in the pecking order, one's identity. There were unspoken limits, which took me some time to decode, as to what was permissible. Wrongly, I at first treated this wary table-talk as a joke – my tart remarks about its 'high level' must have been insufferable – until I realised, to some extent too late, how hurt the others were. It was hard to accept that the talk, stiffly conducted at the long tables, was intended, first and foremost, to show that you respected the code, and only secondly to establish your position within its terms. Above all you must be subservient to its subtle, intransigent values. In the Gorbals this purpose was unknown; our youthful talk, in the shower-room group at the baths for instance, aimed at clearing doubts about the puzzling and impatient world, always concrete; here, that purpose was treated as 'cocky', the presumptuous baring of the soul, better suited to the intimacy of late-night talk with trusted friends.

At every meal you were on show – 'on parade', as the army would put it – giving a good account of yourself. Here too, the others seemed so much better practised.

Perhaps the greatest revelation came from seeing my name up on the tally of rooms – a label on this new life. That, and the fact that wherever you went, people called you sir! I had never thought of myself as a 'sir' before. The others, some not yet used to daily shaving, yet addressed as 'sir' simply because they were students, took the mark of authority as their due. Seemingly, because they *expected* to be treated as important, in this and many other ways, so indeed they were! Why, I wondered, should striplings of seventeen or eighteen receive such respect from men old enough to be their fathers, even their grandfathers! There was something wrong in such a society. Each time I was 'sirred' – actually or figuratively – I felt I must look at myself afresh, as one does in a mirror at random, in case my image had changed unawares; but as time went on, secretly, ashamed, I welcomed such signs that I was 'fitting in', even though part of me despised them.

Another surprise was the ritual of sending notes – invitations to tea or some other social meeting – often on embossed gold-edged cards in creamy, parchment envelopes. Here was an unbelievable, courtly stiffness compared with the Gorbals where, if you wanted to see someone, you climbed up the tenement steps and 'chapped' on the door! In Oxford few people lived further than a short bicycle ride from almost any part of the college area, and there seemed no practical reason for the formality. When I first went to my pigeon hole and found a small square envelope, crested, containing a gold-edged card inviting me to tea at Somerville, I wondered: 'Why spend all this money to ask me to come in for a cup of tea?' And then: 'Must I reply in the same way? Probably yes – or she'll think I don't know how to behave!' The card itself, nearly as stiff as a piece of wood, must have cost as much as the tea! That, I would see as time went by, was not the point. Social discipline was the point, useful when you came to think of it; privacy and personal sovereignty went hand in hand, especially if, for reasons of finesse or caution, you wanted to keep the world at arm's length. After all, it was far easier to dissemble by correspondence than face to face!

Of course, being invited for tea meant more than a simple cup of tea, possibly in a chipped cup, as it would have done in the Gorbals. There were cucumber sandwiches of wafer-thin bread – in winter, anchovy toast – and tea in fine china edged in gold, cream sandwich biscuits and rich fruit cake, almost a meal in itself; afternoon tea, as the genteel folk in Glasgow called it, that I had previously seen only from a distance, standing in the street with nose pressed against the windows of Crawford's tea rooms.

Those cards and little notes, messages of propriety – as well as 'sir' and the like – signalled two things that I learned slowly, too slowly: the importance of ceremony in this new life, and that I must behave as if I really was someone of importance! The others imposed that view of themselves – unthinkingly perhaps, but they did! – so why shouldn't I? But it was a lesson hard to remember.

More painful was the other lesson: that the polite niceties – 'Kelvinside', as we called such behaviour in the Gorbals – were a necessary stage between formal acquaintance and friendship, and that it was unwise, even dangerous, to confuse the two. In the Gorbals they were subtly, intuitively separated, a process that this upper-class politeness – with its refined and in some ways misleading usages – made much more difficult, at least for me; in the Gorbals, 'Kelvinside' was treated as hypocrisy, not to be trusted. Hard to stomach, too, was the thought that these public school folk sailed through it all without effort – the meretricious codes had been learnt long ago.

Less worrying, but startling for a time, was that the word 'work' meant something dramatically different here. Someone would say 'I must get back to my rooms, I have some work to do' – meaning some reading. For me, work and play had changed places. In the factory, work meant the back-breaking routine of lifting and banging and delicately manoeuvring the eighteen-pound press iron on the garments, so that heat and steam and pressure should fix the layers of cloth and canvas in permanent adhesion and shape, and regularly heaving the cooled iron in an arc at waist height from its steel rest-plate beside the pressing donkey over to the gas-fired heating ovens standing against the bare brick wall behind me, the actions endlessly renewed, my clothes soaked in sweat, the noise and steam, and the drumming of the powered sewing machines enclosing me totally – a hermetic life in hermetic toil. For the rest, in the hours of choice, 'play' – or rather escape – meant going to the Mitchell Library to read. Even though in time I, too, adopting some of the protective colouring of this place, would refer to reading books and essay writing as work, that would not be true, for I never felt it as a burden or a worry – perhaps because, as John Buyers of Glasgow University had said in a report on me, I enjoyed the intellectual chase, a chase of ideas, the lure of new horizons. In truth it was essentially the same quest, now, that drew me to teach myself to sail a dinghy, play tennis and squash, punt straight, dance the waltz and the foxtrot and tango – to explore the Aladdin's Cave that Oxford was, the riches so numerous, the choices exhilarating, where the major burden was choice itself.

'And we shall all the pleasures prove . . .'

I learnt to lounge in Fuller's in the Cornmarket of a morning, to linger over coffee and talk – learning the paces and poses of the *boulevardier*, considering the girls, showing one's plumage, testing the signs that could lead to the intimate walk by the river or, later, the sylvan privacy, unchaperoned, of Wytham Woods. The life of the *flaneur* was sweet.

One day, alone for a moment in a girl's room in Lady Margaret Hall – she had gone to fetch a tea-pot from along the corridor – I saw that she had left her diary open, it seemed deliberately, and I saw my name and the words 'he is a glorious young animal!' When she returned I wondered if she read the blushes in my face. 'Glorious young animal' was a modish phrase among her smart set – a cant way of presenting the

Lawrentian, earthy image so much talked about. That, for her, and for others like her, seemed to be how my Gorbals crudeness was interpreted! This, in its way, was a shock too, for I saw nothing glorious in my own vision of myself, such as it was. Still, she had written it approvingly. That must surely be good enough for me too – one area of my Gorbals persona that I need not hasten to change.

To enjoy its sweetness, I must have dimly realised, would conflict with what I thought was the most urgent task, to adopt the Oxford persona as I crudely understood it; but that obsession persisted. Only in retrospect, long after I left Oxford, would I see that quest as misleading and irrelevant, that I must necessarily remain what in the heart of me I truly was; and that the really important task was to discover *that* identity – and let it speak.

3

Crossman: the Game and the Power

Richard Crossman was presiding over a study group on social mobility – upward of course! – a favourite hobby horse of Oxford progressives in those closing days of the Thirties. There were about twenty of us. Most of the others wore loose tweed jackets and flannel trousers – Oxford bags – in varying shades of grey or dark blue, white cotton shirts and college ties; a few wore silk shirts in pastel shades and loosely knotted ties of Shantung silk in glowing colours. I felt staidly overdressed in my grey worsted suit, my only one, bought in Burtons for fifty shillings immediately before leaving Glasgow; I had borrowed the money from Aunt Rachel, and repaid her, for this and other pre-departure loans, out of the first instalment of my scholarship money, received when I arrived in Oxford. As soon as I dared spend more money I would adopt the uniform of tweed jacket and bags.

The square oak panelled room was hung with shafts of moted sunlight. A distant, dreamy murmur, as of lethargic late season insects, gently reminded one of a world outside. Round the walls stood tall book cabinets of dark oak, their leather-bound contents guarded by grilles of thick brass wire. Windows with small leaded panes looked out on a quiet college garden, whose high wall of sand-coloured Cotswold stone was pitted and streaked with slate and iron, and curtained with creepers turning red; the boughs of a solitary pear tree, heavy with late fruit, slanted down, and a few rose bushes bravely held their colours high – blood red, gold, and delicate white – in the slanting autumn sunlight. In this unfamiliar quietude, an ambience that spoke of careful, unhurried measure, I reminded myself over and over again – as if I needed a Spartan corrective of opposites – of the world I had so recently left, the clangour and steam of the factory, the fierce pace of piece work, heaving and banging the eighteen-pound press iron from dark in the early morning to dark in the night, the hermetic greyness of the Gorbals.

Crossman was beautifully groomed, in silver grey suit and dove grey silk tie, in pointed contrast with his turnout when he addressed left-wing meetings at the Plain – shabby flannels, a tweed jacket with leather patches at the elbows, grey or dun shirt and red tie, straight grizzled hair in disarray – which he must have thought gave him a proletarian appearance.

He strained forward in a leather wing chair in a posture suggesting youthful eagerness, twinkled at us through thick-framed glasses. Suave, brilliant, he shot out provocative questions, intervened to sharpen concepts and pose alternative definitions, threw new topics into the discussion, playing us as a conductor played an orchestra. Suddenly, with a lift of the chin that signalled a shaft to the very heart of the matter, he demanded: 'Why do people work?'

Fresh from the Gorbals, I must have become unbearably galled by what I felt to be dilettante arrogance in him, and in the others. Despite total ignorance of life in the lower depths – what it was like to starve or go wet-shod in the rain – how could they talk of the proletarian condition with such total assurance? There was an added irony. Here was I, the one person among them who did know, who carried the marks in my heart and on my hands, and I did not know how to make them see any of it. There were no common points of reference; and words themselves were deficient. To have no money, for instance, no money at all, was to them inconceivable. How *could* they ask, so innocently, 'Why do people work?' I said, curtly: 'Because they'd starve if they didn't!'

Partly I *chose* to misunderstand him, partly I was too angry to look at his question calmly, aware that for them it was in truth academic. I wanted them to hear a note of protest, and pause, and think. Even as I spoke, I knew the words were futile. What I did not bargain for, ignorant of Oxford's capacity for meanness of spirit, was that, in the smoothest possible fashion, Crossman would first patronise me, snub me, and then seek revenge. Revenge? Against whom? A youngster in his first term, totally insignificant!

He stared at me, the smile lines at the side of his mouth fading; then, practised performer that he was, the smile returned. A gasp had gone through the room, and there was a stiffening, a sense of the others drawing away from me. I had committed a gaffe. From my lowly level, Crossman was an important figure, entitled at the very least to ritual respect. Behind the Wykehamist polish, the seemingly careless charm, resided a flinty *hauteur*, dangerous to challenge. Like other middle-class progressives he might pretend to treat you as if you were an equal, but you must not behave as if you really were. I had presumed. I had told him to come down to earth, no longer to look upon the workers as ideological concepts or as the raw material with which to make his way in politics, but as real people, for whom the choices implied in his question seldom existed. Behind his unwillingness to do that lay moral laziness and hypocrisy, and these I had exposed; the full import of my words had probably been missed by the others in the room, but *he* had understood it very well, too well. My shaft had found its mark, and could not be forgiven.

In another fashion, that I could not possibly have understood so early in my time in this new world, I had been even more unwise. The others in that room were part of the new leftwards drift among the middle and upper classes. This new love affair with the virtuous sons of toil, often dismissed as slumming – or by hard-line Marxists as class guilt – was probably an intuitive recognition of a Hegelian wave of social change. Technology was about to extend choices and expectations down to the very base of the social pyramid, and mass opinion would become too powerful to be controlled by traditional loyalties. This was a time to join the masses – or appear to – and *maintain control by leading them*, while you had the chance. Earnestly copying cloth-cap attitudes, these defectors also shared, vicariously, the satisfaction felt by working-class socialists when members of the boss class were won over. Such converts must be treated gently, their blind spots pardoned, lest they retreat to the comfort of their own kind. For such people simply to recognise class injustice was surely all that was required of them? Their witness might convince others of the rightness of the workers' cause. Crossman was such a defector. In making him lose face I had upset the others too.

Having begun as an ardent Platonist, Crossman was in those days still enough of a pure intellectual to enjoy playing with definitions; but of course they had to have social significance. It was in keeping with the spirit of the place. 'Get your concepts clear!' was a prime catch phrase in hall and common room. Here, for Crossman, was an endlessly absorbing intellectual game, to set us analysing fashionable abstractions: 'express the personality through work', 'distinguish between personal fulfilment and "class fulfilment" in the sense of Veblen's conspicuous expenditure', 'work is a means of moral uplift' – the Fabian credo of progress through commitment. The voices of Ruskin and Morris were still influential in Oxford.

Green as I was, such theorising seemed far above in the clouds. I was, in effect, accusing him of hypocrisy, of *pretending* to address important questions while in reality keeping them at a distance.

As for the others, their hurt was plain too. After all, it was 'in' to attend study groups of this kind. They trimmed to the *zeitgeist*, a sure instinct for some of them; on their return from the war they would go into politics. I wanted to expose their smug assumption that the divide between them and the workers could be bridged simply by passionate avowals of unity of interest. As Crossman would demonstrate in his later career, the game, and the power, was what such avowals meant to him, and by inference to others like him.

I must have sensed this disingenuous, repellent quality in the Oxford atmosphere quite early. At first I thought I must be mistaken. Might it be some esoteric joke? If not, how could decent people be so cynical? It would be some time before I understood, with shame, how naive I had been.

Crossman, the smile hanging on his face like a mask, said: 'Of course you're absolutely right! But do tell us, take your father for instance, what made him choose *his* profession?'

'Profession? I don't know if you'd call it that. He learnt the bone-and-wood-turning trade. I suppose *his* father just put him into it, like my father put me into a barber shop to be a soap boy.'

'A soap boy! How fascinating!' The face seemed to light up in genuinely friendly interest, the smile lines beside the mouth seeming to deepen; but behind the heavy spectacles I saw cool reckoning. 'Do tell us about it.'

I described the job; 'and then he put me to the pressing.'

'Pressing? You *must* tell us more. This is *so* interesting.'

I wanted to believe in the apparent warmth, but some genie told me to fear it. I was to learn, painfully, that '*so* interesting' was code for 'I am humouring you while I decide whether it suits me to put up with you any further.' In its many permutations the code would deceive me again and again. The time would come when I would read it effortlessly; and even, God forgive me, use it myself.

Stupidly, thinking they did want to know, I gave a detailed account. The group listened, politely simulating interest. Some may have been fascinated in spite of themselves, and yet, too disturbed by the picture I painted, they were impatient to move away from it. Crossman put his chin in his hands and leaned closer. I could feel the needle-sharp mind acutely focussed, almost hear the scratch of pen on paper within, taking careful notes – grist to his political mill.

Somebody interjected: 'You're making it up! If you had left school at fourteen you couldn't have come up here at all. Pull the other one!'

Crossman was smiling broadly now, no longer wearing the frozen mask of affability. This new smile, I would learn, the bluff hand on the shoulder, indicated satisfaction at having settled something in his mind, some ploy or scheme he would use to his profit. I was of no further interest. 'I want to hear so much more,' he told me. 'Yours is such a remarkable achievement. And such a valuable object lesson for our study of social mobility!'

Addressing the group again, he repeated the question 'Why do people work', as though I had not spoken, but with cloyingly flattering references to my having come up here from the Gorbals. In the code he was saying to me 'Now, be a good fellow and don't bother me any more.'

To patronise you was one of Oxford's favourite ways of responding to someone who came, as I did, from a world whose truths were disturbing. I would suffer months of it, retrospectively burning with shame, until I learned to identify it promptly. With a pretence of interest and regard, and the appearance of welcome, the newcomer was kept at a safe distance, encouraged to lower his guard, to delay his awakening to their indifference or antipathy.

The mandarins prided themselves on their sensibility, but sometimes their lack of it – worn so arrogantly that I wondered whether it was deliberate – appeared in grotesque style. One day an invitation came, gold-edged, embossed, to a *conversazione* at Balliol 'to extend support' to Basque refugee children still being cared for in Britain by a committee of distinguished do-gooders. I looked at the card mystified. I had no contact with any such cause. From curiosity I sent my acceptance. When I arrived, the Master, A. D. Lindsay – later Lord Lindsay – whom I had never met before, wrung my hand, his ruddy smile emollient, clerical:

'*So* helpful of you to come! Our friends from Spain *will* appreciate meeting someone like you with a similar background – you will understand each other so well.'

He led me round the room, a prize working-class exhibit, as if to declare: 'Who says we are out of touch with the workers!'

It was too late to retreat. I knew not a word of Spanish, and the 'children' – some looked older than me – spoke no English, which was perhaps a mercy. They huddled together defensively, regarding us with wonder, searching faces for some hint as to what role we expected of them. I stood sipping tea from a gold-rimmed bone china cup, feeling isolated both from these 'guests' on the one hand and the group of North Oxford notables on the other, and tried to smile at everyone. A strapping girl of about fifteen, with great sad eyes like darkened lamps, and high arched brows, was cajoled into playing a guitar, and some of her companions joined her in chanting a dreamy, meandering tune. Then a few young children, shepherded round a grand piano, sang what sounded like a march. I noticed Lindsay glancing angrily out of the window. Some undergraduates were marching round the quad loudly singing 'Arriba Espana' and waving a Franco flag.

4

Buchenwald on the Tennis Court

Others who brought unwelcome truths were the refugees from Germany.

Reports about Nazi bestiality, the concentration camps, and the flow of refugees from Germany, were complacently dismissed. The Germans were civilised and cultured people, surely incapable of such deeds. The Brownshirts might just possibly do a few unpleasant things, but these were inevitable in changing times. After all, was not Hitler raising up his country and restoring its pride after its humiliation by Britain and France and America? His antics, of course, could be tiresome, but were not to be taken too seriously. At parties someone would slick his hair down over one eye, smear a patch of black on his upper lip from the coal in the grate, and strut about shouting in Teutonic tones: 'Vee must haf Lebensraum!' amid delighted laughter.

The word refugee had meant nothing to me till one harrowing night in the Gorbals, just before Bernard left to fight in Spain, when he had raged about the atrocities against Jews in Germany. One feature caused me particular revulsion; refugees who had been concentration camp prisoners had numbers tattooed on their arms. 'Think of it. Numbers, not people any more!' His words had etched themselves into my soul.

It had been a time of troubled self-enquiry for us both. Certainly that night was memorable. Bernard, my closest friend, went away to Spain. I agonised over whether to do the same. It was a time when the romantic gesture seemed natural. Despite the hideous facts about the Great War, we did not believe they could ever refer to *us* if we shouldered arms. Youth knows it is immortal. Bernard intended to strengthen his communist faith with blood; at least *he* had a cause to fight for! I had none. My passion to break out of the Gorbals was all-consuming. Almost any cause would have done. It was a nice balance. If I had followed Bernard, if I had gone *anywhere*, it would in a sense have been for the wrong reason. That, obscurely, I already knew. The same emotions, whether they were 'wrong' too I would never know, would make me shoot an arrow into the blue and enter the essay competition and, miraculously, win the Oxford scholarship. Inexplicably, my thoughts about escape – the unanswerable question, which was the 'true' escape – were linked with that apocalyptic discussion with Bernard before he went away, and therefore joined, also, to thoughts of tattooed refugees forever carrying the mark of their savage herdsmen, never to be free of them however far they fled; as, perhaps, I would never be free of the Gorbals. Ever afterwards the word refugee triggered the memory of that night when Bernard went away, and the Furies would decide which way I should go.

Thoughts of refugees also upset me for other reasons, properly understood much later. Anti-semitism in the Gorbals, though far from as violent and as publicly condoned as in our parents' countries of origin, oppressed us always, burdened as we were by memories, retailed to us as children by the elders, of relentless persecution – pervasive injustice and humiliation, pogroms, rapes, floggings. Many of us felt driven to flee the whole miserable tradition, to cease to be Jews. This was not *spiritual* revolt in the religious sense. Few of us understood the need for spiritual props, or indeed what they were. 'You work hard, you do the best you can with life – what else is there?' That was the mood of the age but we did not know it. There was certainly no thought of conversion, only a blind urge to shed an identity that burdened every step of our lives, or at least to bury it beneath some protective colouring, so that we might go our private ways like everybody else. A difficult test would come later, with the birth of Israel. For me, coming to Oxford was part of the fantasy escape from being a Jew, yet hardly had I settled in here than reality made me question this too. The refugees I now increasingly heard about, and soon began to meet, were Jews, and in each I saw a disturbing image of the identity I was trying to shed, and was assailed by guilt for wanting to do so. I was betraying them. Their very presence was a reproach.

My first meeting with a refugee took place, ironically I thought, at the tennis courts, in a tranquil setting of trees and rhododendrons, with the slow waters of the Cherwell, tinted green by the reflected foliage, beyond the boundary wire.

I came to be there – I had never wielded a tennis racket before – in the course of trying to solve a prime problem Oxford presented, namely, time. This was something I had never expected. I knew that I would have to break down the Gorbals persona and build anew, but not that it would cling so tenaciously. The use of time was crucial. There was so *much* time. In Glasgow I had longed to be free of the factory so that I could stay in the Mitchell Library, or in the Art Gallery making pencil copies of pictures, as long as I wished. Now that the whole of the day was mine it worried me to find that I lacked the experience, or the training, to use it properly. The nearest to the imposed discipline of the factory was going to lectures. When I first met my tutor I asked him what lectures I should attend. Too timid to ask outright, I wanted help in getting the best out of all this time.

He was astonished. 'My dear fellow, you must sort that out for yourself. You'll find the lectures listed. You can attend the lot if you want to – or none at all – so long as you present your essays promptly, and satisfy me that you have done the reading and the thinking expected of you.'

His response, letting me sink or swim, was probably sound, but at the time it felt brutal. I had hoped for the guidance I had lacked in those hungry hours and days and years in the Mitchell Library. They must have been the richest I would ever know; with help, how much richer might they have been?

Now that I could go to the Bodleian whenever I wished and read all day if I liked, the will to use all these empty hours was fickle. Wanting to reach out for so much, I fretted and fidgeted, and time trickled away.

Accustomed to the sharp-edged air blowing up the Clyde from the sea, in the sluggish, marshy climate of Oxford I found it hard to stay awake, especially in the afternoon, when even the hard wooden chairs in the Radcliffe Camera failed to keep you alert, and a half-hour could be spent staring unseeingly at one page of a book. No wonder the place was nearly deserted then. After lunch it seemed that the entire college streamed out of the gates in games kit. That must be the thing to do, to defeat torpor with hearty exercise. I must find a game I could learn quickly on my own. I bought the cheapest tennis racket I could find, a box of balls, white shorts and white tennis shoes. I decided not to risk buying a special white shirt and white socks. That might tempt providence; I might never learn to play properly. As I donned my new games clothes, the first I had ever owned, symbols of luxury and privilege, my Gorbals self nudged me, as he would again and again for a long time to come: 'Is it really *you* doing this?'

The hard courts, of a smooth green porous substance on which the white markings gleamed luminously, stretched in a long line, with the Cherwell on one side at the foot of a sloping bank of glossy green shrubbery, and a row of poplars on the other. At one end, the main entrance, was a squat brick building, the squash courts, and at the other a timber boat house half-buried in shrubbery and overhung by willows, its peeling green paint betraying slow dissolution in long sleepy summer days. On this November day there was no one on the tennis courts, but in an open gravelled space beside the squash court building a man was hitting a tennis ball against a side wall of it, maintaining a rally on his own. I had seen him at sherry parties, noticeable partly because he was older than the rest of us – he looked about forty – and because of a certain air of detachment, of being ill at ease, that chimed with my own sense of being a stranger within the gates. He was short and somewhat tubby, with sallow features, dark receding hair brushed flat straight back from the brow. Whenever I had seen him he had worn a grey flannel suit, to my experienced eye the work of a high-class bespoke tailor, with real button-holes at the cuffs. Today he was in white flannels with a knife-edge crease, crisp white shirt with short sleeves, grey socks and tennis shoes with thick soles. His smart tennis trousers diminished me somewhat, but the grey socks were consoling.

I walked across the court nearest him and stood by the wire boundary fence pretending to contemplate the river below, and studied the precision and economy of movement as he made each stroke, the grace with which he swivelled and balanced his body to position himself for the return. As with all good players, the skill appeared effortless. Still, I could learn. However it would not do to go over there and try to copy him; in my rawness it would be silly, even embarrassing. I walked along the line of courts till I reached the furthest one, hung my jacket on a hook on the boundary fence, opened the box of balls and threw one high above my head as I had watched others do, and hit it over the net to the further court, hit another, and another, till I had sent over all six, then walked round to the far service line and hit them back again; and so, going back and forth over and over again, I began to get the feel of the racket, featherlight in my calloused palm, and to judge the arc of swing needed to aim the ball.

The strangeness of this new life had a way of striking home at unexpected moments. And now, at the service line again, ready to toss the ball in the air and swing the racket up, something made me halt and be still. I felt the shock of new vision, as when one breasts a mountain ridge and sees a newborn world in its completeness. It seemed that I was lifted up by the thin gleams of sunlight and floated with them as they slanted low through the sombre poplars. I felt the touch of the light breeze on the dark waters passing by. The enveloping quietude was not broken by the harp-like twang of the solitary player's racket or the thwack of tennis ball on brick, but joined and absorbed them. I looked about me, and would not have been surprised to find this sleepy insouciant world replaced with grimy Gorbals streets and black tenements, the roar of Dixon's Blazes beneath the plume of orange flame slanting from the chimney stack. Yes, it was true. I really was here. There was an astringent exultation, a mystic communication from the sinews and the soul, the first awareness, still to be accepted, that the days of heaving the eighteen-pound press iron were behind me.

I resumed my practice. When I was getting five out of six deliveries into the far service court, I felt there was hope.

A voice hailed me: 'Would you care for a game?'

I had forgotten the solitary player. He walked towards me, amiably swiping the air with his racket.

'I can't play!' I said. 'As you can see. In fact this is my first time on a court.'

'Oh, I don't know. Anyway, if you do not expect anyone to join you, we could have a knock-up? Werner Grenz,' he announced, with a stiffening of the back and a slight inclination of the head, and offered his hand.

He was obviously a little out of condition – I put this down to age – for he seemed short of breath when he ran for a ball; but this was not often, for he was so skilled in anticipation and moving into position that he usually seemed to *wait* for the ball to reach him, poised for the stroke, in exactly the right spot. I marvelled at his patience with my wild returns. After about half-an-hour, the light passing into autumn greyness, by tacit agreement we stopped, collected the balls, and strolled in meditative silence to where our jackets, and his white sweater, hung on hooks high on the netting. As he reached up for his sweater, I saw on his left forearm a line of thin blue marks. This was my first sight of Nazi tattooing, but I *knew*. I was hot from exertion, but a chill swept through me, the flesh contracting in goose pimples. An awed fascination made me ask: 'What are those numbers?'

He had begun to draw the sweater over his head, and his face was hidden. He must have answered the question many times. When his face emerged, the cordial expression had changed to blank fixity: 'My concentration camp number.' His eyes searched my face, seeming to say: 'How could you, a Jew, not know that?'

Bernard's words rang in my head: 'Think of it – numbers! Not people any more.'

Stupidly, I blurted out, 'Which one?'

Later, alone, I blushed at my question, as one might ask someone at a party: 'What college?'

'Buchenwald.'

In the stillness of the early evening we walked out of the courts without speaking, along quiet roads lined by detached brick houses set well back behind glistening evergreens and close-set board fencing. Tall sash windows on the raised ground floors, hung with gathered lace curtains, glowed yellow from table lamps with large drum-shaped parchment shades. From one house came the sound of a flute, pure, precise, detached, suggesting Vivaldi. In another someone picked out on a piano something of Bach. No cars passed. Now and then a creaking sound, as of metal dragged along the ground, slowly approached, and a student rode by on an old 'sit-up-and-beg' bicycle from whose handlebars a wicker basket hung, swaying from side to side with the effort of pushing the complaining chain round, gown swishing behind him.

Press and radio, as we learned in later years, had clouded or suppressed reports of the camps, but we did know the names of Buchenwald and Dachau; and while none of us knew with certainty what went on there, the fact that people were being herded into them like animals was horror enough. Dehumanisation as an instrument of state policy was yet to become familiar, but its practice, already sensed, lay heavy on the heart. Unimaginable, I yet tried to imagine what the camps were like, with little to go on except films and books about prisoners of war in the Great War – grey-faced people clutching a few belongings, the mud and the cold, stark huts, barbed wire, brutal guards.

Buchenwald. Now that I had made him say the word, I looked at the quiet tree-lined road, everything in it speaking of comfort, ordered living, secure horizons, and was filled with sadness. How could there be such serenity when Buchenwald existed? These houses should burst open with grief – or at least show their awareness, their revulsion, by even one break in this composure! Why did the sky not open up and a great cry come down from on high?

Yet who was I to judge this world behind its lace curtains? I too was trying hard not to be touched.

Feeling inadequate, I said, 'You are the first I've met. I'm sorry.'

He nodded, looking straight ahead, and remained silent.

After a minute or so he began to talk, at first stiffly, grudgingly; and then, perhaps sensing how upset I was, more easily. A biochemist, he had been forced out of his research post at Berlin and sent to Buchenwald. He was in Oxford at the invitation of a committee for refugee scientists, but he had been waiting for two months and the expected offer of a post had not come.

I asked, 'How did you get out?'

Instead of answering, he asked, 'Where do you come from?'

'Glasgow.'

He shook his head, as if I had answered the wrong question: 'And your family? They are not surely from this country?'

An imperious quality in his voice nettled me. I countered with a question: 'How can you tell?'

Why did I resent his unerring perception that I was a Jew? And then I saw it, something that spoke from deep within him, or rather through him, mysterious, powerful, inescapable, buried far away in history, a demand that I honour an ancient bond.

How ironic that this voice should speak now, when I sought to shed the identity? Or was it rather the bond I wanted to disown? It was a bond in more than one sense; it had bound us together through the ages, from the days in Egypt and Babylon, assailed by prejudice and the self-doubt of many faiths. In our shower-room group in the Gorbals baths we often said: 'If the Jews weren't persecuted they'd be assimilated out of existence in no time! If only they [the persecutors] understood that, they'd have got rid of us long ago!'

However good his protective colouring, did some self-punishing impulse make the Jew reveal himself unawares, perhaps in defiance? If that impulse was working within *me* I must root it out. Perhaps the only cure was to destroy the sentiments that defined you as a Jew *to yourself*, the urge to treasure a secret identity, uphold traditions that attracted hate? Pride in being a Jew was a dangerous luxury.

That was a way of putting it, suiting the embattled spirit. It settled nothing. It raised other demons. If it was too painful to be a Jew, and if I was an outsider not only in the Gorbals but here in Oxford too, where *could* I belong? 'Wait,' I told myself; 'it's too soon to say that – you haven't given this new life a chance!'

Werner seemed lost in thought; he may not have heard my question, or more probably, felt it was unimportant. At last he said, as if pursuing a thought aloud, 'My family in the days of the Kaiser were *Hofjuden*.' He looked at me closely, searching for an expected response. He raised his shoulders. 'And now this is where I am!'

'Talking to me, you mean?'

I was ashamed. How could I be so boorish?

Many years later, in some ways too late, I would see that my obsessive worries about belonging, about shedding Jewish identity, though in themselves important, were only symptoms of that oceanic disquiet natural to this phase between adolescence and maturity, especially at a place like Oxford. Ceaselessly you harrowed the spirit with questions about religion and final ends, closely related to concern with personal worth. You were driven by heightened sensibility to regard every detail of your response to the world, every shift in the responses of others to *you*, as a comment on your own fledgling solidity. You felt vulnerable much of the time. In this extreme of self-regard I had been stung by something in his manner – the word *Hofjuden* meant nothing to me – suggesting that he was an aristocrat talking down to me.

A flush suffused his sallow features: 'You misunderstand me. I was thinking about the change in my circumstances. Our position, what we have contributed to our country, Germany – after all, we thought of it as our country – it is all gone for nothing, *finished*. As if it had never been. You see? That is it.'

'What are *Hofjuden?*'

'Ah – you do not know? I thought you would have – well, never mind. I will tell you. *Hofjuden* were Jews who were recognised by the royal court. They had status. They were *Juden* – I mean Jews – who were what you would call here the upper class? I do not mean to be impolite. I simply state facts. Our family were bankers, merchants, important business people. In those old days of my grandfather some were in the army as officers. We moved at a certain level of society.'

He looked away, perhaps in delicacy.

I told him my parents had come from Lithuania.

'Ah yes, Litvaks!' He nodded to himself as if confirming a judgment.

It was easy to see what it was. There had been no *Hofjuden* where my family had come from. From Germany, he told me, few if any *Hofjuden* had emigrated; in those far-off days they had felt secure. Emigrant Jews were the poor. I was not of his class.

After a silence he said: 'Forgive me, when I referred to your family as Litvaks I meant no disparagement, you understand? In the old Pale of Settlement days things were bad for the Jews, but at least there was no *pretence*. The Jews there *knew* they had no secure place. They knew where they stood. In the old Germany we thought we did have a place. That is why for us the shock is greater.'

His words, suavely dismissive now, sustaining his position, spurred me to look for weaknesses: 'How Jewish were you?'

Again I felt ashamed. Who was I to weigh the worth of *his* Jewishness – anyone's?

He drew in his breath sharply: 'We were not observant. We were, you know, three times a year Jews, Rosh Hashonoh and Yom Kippur Jews – that and Bar Mitzvah and so on. But we were openly *known* as Jews. We thought . . .' He shrugged. 'We thought of ourselves as really no different from people who were – what shall I say – who were known as Lutherans or Roman Catholics. Normal people! That was what we thought. It is hard to believe it now. Life was good. We felt secure. We belonged to a civilised, cultured society. How could that ever change? And then it was as though all that had been a dream. The old poison re-appeared in full force. We had been blind. We thought it could not touch *us!*'

'Did all your family get out?'

He did not reply at once. 'What did you say? I am sorry, my thoughts slipped away.'

'Your family, where are they?'

'They are in the States now. My wife and children; my father and mother, uncles and their families. Yes, thank God. We all got away, perhaps just in time. As for me, if the offer here does not materialise soon I shall go on to the States myself.'

Bitterness returned; here was another one who had only to make up his mind: 'I'll go . . .' and the money was there, ready to hand. Would I ever stop envying people who could do that? The thought slipped out: 'At least you've got the money to go where you want to.'

'Of course! That is to say, we *had*.' He looked at me narrowly. 'Let us say we were reasonably well off. Now it is different. Most of it has gone, partly with confiscation, or what amounts to that – forced sale of assets for a few pfennigs. The price of our lives. Partly in bribing people, to get out of Buchenwald, to get papers and so on. We did get some of it out but –' he shrugged '– not much.'

Not much? Here was yet another lesson in the bizarre values of this place. 'Not much', in Oxford language, would mean riches to me. If I heard someone say 'I haven't any money', he did not mean that he literally had not a single penny to his name – as I would if I said it – but that his allowance would not stretch to something he particularly wanted to do; a slight inconvenience, a matter of asking family or trustees for more cash, or waiting until he could draw on the next ample remittance.

I said: 'And what about all the others?'

He halted, scrutinised me again, then turned away: 'I know who you mean.' His thin lips drew tight. 'The people who cannot buy their way out. Yes, it is true. For them it is bad – very bad.'

I thought of Bernard talking about the *guerre kilometrique* that was so near, on that traumatic night on our way to his house, to the sad meal with his dying father who would still affirm that the humane world must soon come into its own, and that our simple task was to hasten that day. I had half-believed him, or rather I had wanted to. Here in the tranquillity of Oxford it was hard to imagine that the *guerre kilometrique* was imminent. If it did come, what fate awaited 'all the rest', the Jews in Germany who could not buy their way out?

It seemed that a cloud of guilt hung round Werner's shoulders and spread out to envelop me also. Was it his fault that *he* could buy his way out? Would I have done the same in his place? It was a hard question. I supposed I would. In a sense I *had*. With my scholarship I had bought my way out of the Gorbals. I had left 'all the rest' to their fate, as Werner

---

had done. No, that was an absurd comparison. Even so, luckier than the people I had left behind, did I go about as he did lamenting my ill-fortune? I hoped not. Then I remembered my self-pity of a few moments before. Who was I to sit in judgment on him?

As if speaking to himself, he said: 'Those others, they will not survive – most of them, I am sure of that.'

I dared not look at him.

No hint of the unthinkable, the Final Solution, was as yet even whispered. Reports of anti-Jewish atrocities in Germany, dismissed as mischievous Zionist fancies, were plausible enough to me; childhood memory, imprinted with stories of pogroms, had incised its lessons deeply. I could not have put a name to what was in store, but I *knew*.

Until this moment, despite the occasional reminder of Bernard's talk of the *guerre kilometrique*, thoughts of a coming war had troubled me little, kept at a distance, perhaps, as I savoured my new world to the full. In unthinking moments, however, walking in Christ Church Meadow, swishing through the fallen leaves, or in hall listening to carefree talk, the outer world would come close and say 'Don't waste time – there's not much left.' Or leaning out of my window in the stillness of the night, pondering upon the stars suspended in a sky of Prussian blue velvet, above a skyline easily imagined as mediaeval – low gables leaning together, irregular roof-lines huddled below unruly steeples – the enigmatic powers hovered near, brooding presences, ageless, savage, unrelenting from century to century, no longer romantically alluring as they had been long ago, when as a child I had sailed out to the galaxies and heard the Sybilline music. There beyond the spellbound roofs lay an infernal horizon where the dogs of war moved steadily nearer. How many days were left? How many moments?

Werner was a messenger of the Fates, a lone symbolic figure projected across Europe, to herald the unthinkable. I knew it in my bones. Yet I could not, would not, hold the thought steadily and look at it.

I had been amazed to hear him talk of the old poison 'returning'. When had it ever gone away? In the Gorbals it had been with us always, contained – at least in its more violent forms – only by frail constraints, mild social disapproval, unease among Christian clergy, wary self-interest in some of the prejudiced, and in recent years the beginnings of organised defiance from Jewish youth. It needed only a beguiling stimulus, which

Mosley looked like providing, to erupt in the savagery from which Werner had escaped. So that too was on its way.

When Bernard had talked of war just round the corner I had believed it intellectually, not in my stomach as I did now. I had needed little urging from him to take up the scholarship and behave as if war was not going to happen. How ironic were the Fates? They had plucked me out of the Gorbals, let me taste this bounteous life, and were now ready to snatch it away. I said to my soul: 'Be still. It is yours. Take it while you can.'

Once again I tried to imagine what awaited the Jews left behind in Germany. Thoughts went back to the old people in the Gorbals talking of pogroms *in der heim*; soldiers rampaging through a ghetto, mediaeval cruelty and ecstasy. Perhaps it had already begun? At a different level, how could I imagine what it was like to lose the security Werner had known – financial, social, and in freedom of choice – when I had never known it myself?

What *ought* I to feel? Thinking of that moment years later, my insensitivity appalled me. Detachment must have been my defence in the Gorbals, and it persisted. My years of Gorbals squalor and closed horizons, all my life so far, must have calloused the soul. I should have understood more, cared more. Petty feelings, like resentment at Werner's condescension, should not have ruled me. For that matter I may even have misunderstood him. Bitter at being here on sufferance, awaiting the favour of a faceless committee, his talk of *Hofjuden*, putting me to the proof of rank, may have been his way of presenting himself at what he took to be *my* level – a conventional Oxford undergraduate of a like social position! I had no idea I played the part so convincingly.

The deserted road skirted the grounds of the University Air Squadron. As we reached the gates the deep rumble of a powerful engine approached from within, and a long boat-shaped Bentley crunched the gravel round a clump of shrubbery and swept out. The driver, about twenty, fair-haired, with a knobbly face, wore a dark grey flannel suit, a shirt with a cutaway collar, a tie of sponge-bag pattern in a massive Windsor knot, and a charcoal grey bowler low over his eyes, a turnout sometimes referred to as the undress uniform of the Brigade.

Werner asked, 'Do you know him – Fiorenza?'

I had heard the name, that of a wealthy Jewish family long settled in this country.

'I've seen the car about,' I said. 'I suppose that's why the face is familiar.'

I remembered something else about him, and without thinking how discordant a note it would strike, I said that I had seen him in the tails and pink facings of the Bollinger.

'Please? What is the Bollinger?'

I told him about the roistering dining club.

He nodded understandingly, even a shade wistfully. 'It is logical after all. You might say that Jews like him are the *Hofjuden* of this country. More English than the English – just as people used to say of *us*, disparagingly, that we were more German than the Germans.'

He was more open now. Something had changed between us. Fiorenza, and the attitudes he exemplified, had brought us closer. Werner must have regarded him with the poignant emotions with which a refugee French aristocrat of the *ancien régime* could have contemplated the insouciance of the English gentry. My own envy, though it sprang from totally different sentiments, must have been clear to him too. Our isolation and doubt, and guilt, were in origin so diverse, but we could share emotional bridges, and our burdens became lighter. In an unspoken compact, we could cautiously lower our defences.

When I knew him well, I would see the sensitivity and compassion beneath the appearance of arrogance. For the present, however, neither of us had any sympathy to spare for the world – and without the need of words we understood this of each other, and accepted it.

He said: 'People like that are putting on the same airs as we did in *our* mistaken sense of security. Look where *we* are now. That is where you too could be, one day.'

'I mean,' he added quickly, 'not you personally of course, but Jews like him who believe the insular English superiority belongs to them too.'

That ultra-Englishness contained a further irony, hidden from us; the model of the Englishman, proconsular, Arnoldian, was already a sunset vision, its reality deep in the past. He said: 'Members of our family, and others like us, served the Emperor – Iron Crosses, other honours. Germany was our country. Our culture. Nothing could touch us! The ghetto was far back in history – we did not look back to it, just as *they* do not.' He gestured to where the Bentley had disappeared from view.

With a wry grimace he told me that some of Fiorenza's relatives in the

City were helping to fund the committee whose decision he was awaiting.

He turned to me, halted, and startled me by bursting out laughing. 'My God, I must stop this. As you English say, pull myself together, no? I tell you what I propose. Let us dine together tonight if you are free? We should look at the bright side, yes?'

The sudden change was a release. I was flattered, too, that this sophisticated, scholarly man should want my company.

'All right. I'd like that.'

Before we parted, he asked: 'You do not go to the University Jewish Society? I have not seen you at meetings? You should go.'

'Frankly, I've been avoiding that sort of contact.'

This was not the time to say that I wanted to stop being a Jew. I was not the only one – Hitler and history had pulled him back into that old identity, and now, paradoxically, he was forced to claim it fully once again, to draw on the compassion of *other* Jews, the historic bond.

He studied me again, deep sadness on the sallow features: 'I think I understand,' he said, 'how you feel about being Jewish, but believe me this is not the time to turn away; to be isolated is the last thing we should wish for at this historic time.'

Stupidly, I would not grasp his meaning. His reference to Fiorenza still hurt. Despite his quick denial he *had* bracketed me with him, no doubt assuming that our attitudes were the same. Arrived here from the lower depths of the Gorbals, what could I have in common with the English *Hofjuden*?

I said: 'The Jewish problem will never go away. Why don't we simply stop being Jews and be done with it?'

'They will not let us! They hunger for the scapegoat of the past. There are such people even here in Oxford. I used to think that in the atmosphere of pure enquiry at a university there could be no prejudice. That was foolishness. Look at that student in Trinity with a swastika flag in his window, and his gramophone booming out the 'Horst Wessel Lied'. Such people will not let you forget your Jewishness – when it suits them. That way, believe me my friend, there is no way out.'

We had halted near the corner of Holywell, where he had rooms above a bespoke shoemaker whose window displayed a sheet of paper with pencilled outlines of the Prince of Wales's feet – apparently the good man did not qualify for the display of the three white feathers. Street lamps glowed, and dim yellow electric light shone in the tall sash windows behind the pillared portico of the Clarendon Building across the way, where the Broad opened wide opposite the Indian Institute and the Bridge of Sighs at the entrance to New College Lane. Bicycles rattled by on every side, some with carbide lamps hissing, the gas acrid in the nostrils, some with dynamo lamps, many with none, the riders' gowns fluttering like witches' cloaks among the glow-worm lights wavering and bobbing. From the far end of the Broad there approached a din of shouting and chanting and a cacophony of bicycle bells. Down past Trinity and Blackwell's, four abreast, rode a group of about twenty young men and women, sounding the bells on their handlebars in shrill chorus, and singing at the top of their voices the Zionist anthem, 'Hatikvah' – Hebrew for 'The hope' – to the melody of a Moldavian folk song: 'Cart and Ox'.

> As long as a Jewish soul
> still yearns in the innermost heart,
> and eyes turn eastward
> gazing towards Zion,
> then our hope is not lost,
> the hope of two thousand years,
> – to be a free people in our land,
> the land of Zion and Jerusalem.

In the middle of the front row two girls led the chanting, their clear silver voices carrying the song up into the sky triumphantly, joyously. Both radiated an energy, a womanly earthiness, that crackled through the dark air and touched my flesh like sparks of static electricity. One of them, buxom, long-legged, had glossy black hair cascading to her shoulders, and pale, finely-drawn olive features; she wore a white blouse embroidered down the front with red flowers and a skirt of claret-coloured velvet that billowed out above a dimpled knee as the pedal reached the top of its circle. The other girl was fair, with full rosy lips, high cheekbones and dazzling white teeth, small waist and wide hips, wearing a long flowing woollen dress in blue and white vertical stripes. Both wore scholar's gowns.

'I see you have good taste in women!' Werner chuckled, smacking his lips. 'Like me, but the less said about that the better. Still, a man must

live, must he not? Those two are leading lights in the Jewish Society –
the dark one is Rachel, and the other is Hannah. A word of advice: they
are firebrands – prophetesses of a Jewish national home in Palestine. My
God, what can one say about that? I cannot see any hope of a Jewish
Palestine. And even if by a miracle it did happen, what are you and I
going to do – you in a mood to discard your Jewishness, and as for me,
I don't know what to say. Do I want to live in a totally Jewish milieu? I'm
not sure I do.'

I said I would go with him to the Jewish Society. He grinned and
slapped my shoulder. 'I will introduce you to those two. It will be
interesting to see what develops. I think I can guess. They will not know
what to make of you, but will be drawn like moths to a candle. But be
careful. That kind could take you up, be amused for a time, and drop
you and move on. Still, who knows?' He shrugged. '*Le coeur a ses raisons*,
eh?' Then he added, slyly, 'Remember my friend, they are *Hofjuden*, the
lot of them. You will learn a lot – maybe not all of it to your liking.'

5

G. D. H. Cole: Fabian Twilight

I never dared ask why I was invited, out of the blue, to join the Cole Group. Later, receiving other such unexpected invitations, and putting together scraps of gossip dropped from high tables and passed along the bush telegraph, I concluded that they must have indirectly resulted from my outburst at Richard Crossman's seminar. Suavely dismissed by him at the time, I had assumed it had been forgotten, but I was wrong. His pride had suffered. I was too inexperienced to know that Oxford luminaries did not feel safe on their Olympian heights but guarded their positions with a million bayonets. Stories about the incident had made the rounds of senior common rooms, undoubtedly spread by Crossman himself, a way of getting revenge in a typically tortuous manner. I had much to learn about Oxford gossip, addictive, obsessional, Byzantine, instrument of manoeuvre and war. That story of the rough young fellow from the Gorbals slums doubtless titillated cloistered superiority and its liking for condescending swordplay; it would be amusing to confront the strange creature – and take him down a peg! Crossman must have reasoned that if I ran true to form, others would lose face as he had done; and in their merciless response yet more bayonets would turn their points towards me. An elegant scheme.

G. D. H. Cole brought together selected people to his rooms, undergraduates and a few senior members of the University, like Patrick Gordon Walker, to discuss, as he put it, evolving socialist policy. In his gradualist idealism there were echoes of Bernard's father, though founded on a richer scholarship. We must emancipate the lower orders through betterment, refined social design to level people upwards, cultural uplift linked to spiritually rewarding work. More humane social principles would raise men and women to the full expression of the personality – a concept I found mystifying; no one paused to define it, and I was ashamed, at that early stage, to ask what they meant by it. What were 'humane' principles? What did expression mean, what *was* the personality, and how did you know when its expression was beneficial, to you or to others? Was all this vagueness deliberate – lest you pin anyone down! That labyrinthine discussion led nowhere. For the Cole Group, and in fairness other 'progressive' gatherings, expression of the personality was simply a comforting shibboleth. There were echoes of Keir Hardie, Paine, Rousseau. Even in his appearance Cole suggested the advanced elite of the turn of the century, Bloomsbury and South Place – well-tailored smooth tweeds, sharp boyish features and fresh complexion hinting at long breezy walks along ley lines, severity of thought, closeness to the lodestone of Nature.

One sensed, in the Group, the feeling that the creed must accommodate to a changed *zeitgeist* impatient with the old, gentle, persuasive posture of socialism; and that it must blunt the aggression of the new radicalism by moving towards it – or appearing to do so. Progressive Oxford still reeled from the shock of *The Road to Wigan Pier*. A visitor from another planet could well have assumed that Oxford had just received reports of the way of life of a little-known breed of person called workers, and that the information had yet to be understood, let alone digested.

I marvelled that *The Road to Wigan Pier*, to me naive, had made such a stir. I could think of nothing in it that was not obvious, but when I said so in the Cole Group it was as if I had uttered a mortal heresy. I forgot that having lived all my life at the lowest level of the pyramid, lower than anywhere Orwell had been – or would have recognised as such if he had – I perceived its characteristics in my heart, not in my mind, with its subtleties of outlook and aspiration, far more clearly than the middle-class voyeur Orwell could. I should have been quicker to understand this at the time. If I had, I would not have been so arrogantly dismissive, so determined on the impossible task of making others see the workers' life truly, when there was no common language, no shared sensibility. Sadly, as the years passed, I would have to accept that my non-conforming vision, whether the effect of heritage or the imprint of the Gorbals or both made no matter, separated me emotionally from 'them' for ever. I could never truly join them, except in specific, personal –and alas often short-lived – felicities; and even these would owe their stimulus, at least for people on the other side of the divide, more to fascination with my differentness than true sympathy. The attempt to 'go native' was doomed from the start. That irony was hidden from me, or I might have fled Oxford there and then.

I had worshipped Cole on the printed page, and my first sight of him in the flesh was fittingly magical. His dark-panelled sitting room, dimly lit by parchment-shaded table lamps, and the leaping flames from heaped coals in a wide stone fireplace, was dominated by the enormous flared and curling horn of a gramophone – suggesting Thor's hunting horn – which rose up to within inches of the ceiling and cast an apocalyptic shadow upon the wall behind his head. Till I arrived in Oxford I had never met anyone who *owned* a gramophone. This one was of the highest class, using fibre stalks as needles, considered a mark of the fastidious mind. Cole sat beneath the horn, enveloped in a deep leather chair, peering over the arm of it, birdlike, a furtive smile on the small, slightly pouting mouth.

I noted the others' technique as they helped themselves to coffee from a silver pot on a wheeled mahogany server, in tiny cups of fine china with minute saucers, used silver tongs to pick sugar lumps from a fluted silver bowl, wedged a small round ginger biscuit between the cup and the steep side of the saucer, and sidled into the crowd. They did these things with automatic ease, but I had to watch and copy as I went, and was slow. Before coming to Oxford I had never tasted coffee, but as in many other untried things – drinking, smoking – I sheepishly followed the mode. Many months would pass before I found coffee palatable, or thought I did. I fancy I told myself it was necessary to enjoy such things – force myself to do so come what may! – if I seriously meant to fit into this new world.

Nor had I mastered the social art of drinking and eating in mid-air, with no solid surface at hand on which to rest cup and saucer. As I moved gingerly into the middle of the room, someone nudged me gently and I barely saved my coffee from spilling; Rachel said at my shoulder: 'How *amusing* to meet you here!'

Werner, true to his promise, had introduced me to her, and to Hannah, at the University Jewish Society. Girls in the university, outnumbered by the men eight to one, were in a buyers' market. These two, signalling to each other in their mysterious feminine code, must have decided that Rachel should sample me first; Hannah's turn would come. Rachel, in her mannered speech – hybrid of Garsington and Mayfair – had confided to me that I was sympathetic. As the next step in the genteel social measure, in a few days I was to go to tea with her, when she would be chaperoned.

The room having filled up, and with the waves of heat from the coal fire, the place was torrid, and her dark odour as she leaned close surged through me, making me breathless. These were child of nature days, new to me; girl undergraduates experimented with the persona of the Lawrentian woman, the earth mother, whose pure, demanding essence, the life force, rightly proclaimed itself in the potent message of her sweat.

The crowd pressing us together, the earthy chemistry took possession. If only I could go – somewhere, anywhere – and take her with me! Social punctilio, I reminded myself, demanded small talk – a skill I had never learned. Unsteadily I said, 'This is an odd place to find you?'

'Good Heavens why?'

I searched for a reply: 'You're not left-wing are you?' That sounded pompous; my attempt to recover was little better. 'The other day you were full of plans for capitalist enterprise, buying land in Palestine for settlers, setting up industries, investments and profit returns and so on. I thought . . .'

'Oh how sweet!' She leaned closer and the siren smell took all sense away; and she, perfectly aware of that, continued with complete composure, saying gently, half-coaxingly, though the words were irrelevant: 'One does have to make things pay, doesn't one? And the idea is joint ownership among us settlers. So we'll *all* be workers then, won't we?'

She smiled half to herself. And I nodded, nothing more needed. We both knew that the words had no purpose but to endorse this contact – every formality, as by a miracle, now stripped away. Signals had been exchanged. We would now move on as if we had known each other for ever. The smile, I knew also, was a reference to the chaperoned tea! That too was now irrelevant. We were content.

A movement in the room told us that the coffee overture was at an end. There was a scraping of chairs. She whispered: 'Let's sit on the floor.'

In the Gorbals, sitting on the floor was not respectable. Apart from gentility, since many tenement dwellers could not afford floor covering, if you sat on the rough planking you might get a nail or a splinter – a 'skelf' – in your bottom, to say nothing of making your clothes dirty. People here seemed deliberately to *choose* the floor as a sign of the free spirit, scoffing at 'stuffiness'. In any case they could afford not to worry about spoiling their clothes.

Cole talked about Fabianism. Cant phrases recurred – social betterment, dignity for the labouring man . . . Change was in the air. How should Fabians respond? Crucially they must not be tempted, moved by compassion, to advocate social changes before the evils they were designed to cure had been fully understood, as well as the distant implications of the 'cures' themselves. An immediate need was to study the challenge presented by *The Road to Wigan Pier*. He turned to me: 'I hear you are from the Gorbals. That is highly interesting; a personal view from such a place would be most valuable. I imagine the conditions are comparable?'

Before I could answer, he went on: 'I wonder if you would care to tell us what you think of Orwell's message?'

Awe of the great man fought with hurt. Seeming to want to hear what I had to say, he was looking far beyond me. The intellectual steamroller moved urbanely, inexorably. I was being used in some way, unrelated to any insights I could offer. I had a feeling they were not desired. Unlike these people, Orwell at least had had the courage to acknowledge his ignorance and try to remedy it.

I said: 'I don't think he *has* any message – except, maybe, a warning that the do-gooders from the boss class should try to understand the workers before it's too late.'

Rachel drew her breath in sharply and I felt the ripple of excitement in her body.

Cole straightened his lean form in the deep chair, the ghost of a smile flickering across the pursed lips. 'That is *most* interesting? Now, do tell us – are the conditions Orwell describes, and the attitudes of the people, a fair representation of working-class life as you knew it in the Gorbals?'

'What do you mean by fair? Some of the people in his book are a damn sight better off.'

He seemed to draw into himself, still considering me with that youthful, open gaze. With a little shake of the head, he said, 'We have a lot to learn from you. But it will take time. We speak, alas, different languages.' He finished with a flicker of a smile.

Unlike Crossman, I felt he was sincere.

It was, surely, hard for these people? I thought of Bernard's father exhorting me to carry the torch. Where in this comfortable, obscurantist preserve would I look for it? Even prophets like Cole were in confusion, skilled though they were in concealing it.

The dusty abstractions were thrown back and forth yet again, a dead language; Benthamite and Platonic formulae, élite condescension: 'we must take culture to the workers', Shakespeare in the valleys. To instil elevated aesthetic sensibility in the workers was a moral imperative.

If Oxford undergraduates played football with unemployed miners a blow was struck for uplift.

The role of prize exhibit, untutored savage from another world, at first beguiling, even a little glamorous, was now spiritually lowering. Even among the tiny sprinkling of working-class students – whom the genteel Glasgow parlance would have described as 'respectable working class' – the Gorbals was regarded as the lowest of the lower depths.

Werner, it was true, was becoming a friend. We met often for knock-ups on the tennis court, and long talks over tea or dinner. His cultivated company, opening up wide new horizons, was stimulating, but in the absence of shared childhood memories, as there had been with Bernard, an indefinable frontier remained closed; I could not talk from the heart. The link with Bernard did continue by letter, but that was no substitute. On paper, thoughts lost the fine touch the emotions needed. There was, however, a ray of hope; Bernard, moving fast up the union ladder, would soon be travelling south from time to time on union business, and we would meet.

As for my family, there had been little enough communication in the past, and now there was nothing to build on. I wrote to father and my sisters, Lilian and Mary, and Aunt Rachel, and got laconic messages back. In my sisters' letters, reading between the lines, I found a self-justifying resentment, the accusation – mystifying to me – that it was I who was guilty of severing the vital links, when in truth it was *they* who had done so long ago when I was a small child; they had gone off on their own after mother's death and left father to cope with me as best he could. Aunt Rachel, mother's sister, sent fragmentary news, of Uncle Salman's declining strength, of familiar hardships, bonds of a kind; there was warmth, but also concern for me, regret, fear. The worry was genuine, there was no doubt of that. I knew that it was doubly charged, as if she tried to give me what mother, dead long ago, could not. I read the letters again and again as I strode furiously across the Parks, and the wind threw tears cold against my face. Often, reading her carefully rounded copperplate English – learnt at night school long ago – I heard again the words she had uttered through tears when I first told her of the scholarship: 'If only your mother could have been spared to see you turn out like this! Her beautiful baby boy she had to leave so soon.' She worried

– as Alec had done but for more profound reasons – seeing her sister's line broken in fragments, that the road I had taken would sever the heart's roots. She tried to extend to me the concern my mother would have shown. I knew that Uncle Salman, seen in the mind's eye forever crouched over his sewing in the little front room workshop, shared her feelings. I would not understand their fear for me till many years of stumbling and picking myself up again had gone by, long after they too were dead; and all I could do in acknowledgment and homage, and futile gratitude, would be to stand at their graves and bare my soul to the wind.

Father's brief lines were full of a sombre perplexity only too familiar. Indirectly, however, they carried a special shock, for to my amazement I had difficulty deciphering the words. He wrote in Yiddish, and following the common practice used the Hebrew cursive script. As a child I had learned to read and write Hebrew and Yiddish fluently; now the knowledge was fading fast. Soon it would be irrecoverable. There indeed was a reminder, like a wind from the icy mountains, of how far I had fled. I was destroying all signs of the way I had come! How many more fierce ironies were in store? Here was Rachel, and so many more, rushing to recapture a fading Jewish identity, and here was I fleeing madly in the opposite direction.

It was a shock to see from such signs, that a demon worked within me in secret, devious, implacable, destined always to get his own way.

Though outwardly gregarious, this new life was lonely. I longed to find one soul with whom I need not be defensive, or alert for pitfalls set by the code, to whom I could open my heart – or so I thought. Bernard had equated the doubt and loneliness of ordinary life with like feelings in the soldier: 'Having a woman gives you back a breath of your own true self.' He had meant much more than sex, as Alec had done in *his* stoic summing up on life: 'Ye go tae wurrk, ye eat a bit, fuck a bit! Whit else is there?' The two voices were not so far apart. As Bernard saw it, renewal through a woman was a Lawrentian key to everything else – to a spiritual balance, a necessary plenitude of feeling. The child of nature vogue, perhaps, had some sense to it after all? When I had come away from Glasgow I had left Bunty behind, Alec's cousin, passionate siren in the factory; she had begged me to let her come south to Oxford with me. She would work hard, care for me, simply to be at my side. No, I had told myself, it would be wrong to make her travel this road with me. How could she? How I had underrated her!

In any case, in the rigidly conventional conditions of Oxford at that time, life with her would have been made unworkable.

And now here beside me was Rachel, who was perhaps even more distant from me in outlook and personality than Bunty – rich, assured, fanatically pursuing a quest that was surely futile – a fantasy, a blind determination to make the Bible come true, against all the historic odds. Was I exchanging one doomed relationship for another? What had I in common with Zionism? Nothing, as Werner observed, but a heavy heart.

A measured, sonorous voice broke into my thoughts. Cole was addressing me again: 'You say we need to learn more about the workers. That observation contains a serious criticism, and you may be right. But tell us, how do you suggest we go about it, since you think that Orwell's effort falls short?'

Anxious to repair my inattention I spoke hastily – too hastily – and my words, encapsulating doubts about myself, the world, the road I was on, took me by surprise: 'That's what I thought I came here to Oxford to find out from people like you.'

I felt my cheeks flush in shame. He looked at me with a kind of wonder, of recognition, as if he remembered a time, long ago, when he had felt an equal disappointment. Softly he said: 'There is a profound irony in what you say. Our task is harder than yours. We need to see the workers as you can; but you can do it *without trying*, as naturally as breathing, encompassing innumerable truths, tiny but vital, at a glance. Alas we cannot. There are many things you could tell us, but you do not know how to – yet. The enlightenment you want from us – and will certainly get if I judge you correctly – conceptual, disciplined, is likely to destroy the freshness of your untutored vision, the unique quality you now possess.'

The openness staggered me, and I almost worshipped him afresh for it. Blinded by knowledge, philosophy, qualification, they saw too little because they knew, or 'saw', too much! They groped about in a fog of knowledge. If the road I was following would do no more than take *me* into that same fog, what was the point?

6

Rachel

Rachel exclaimed: 'My God these Oxford men are *so* juvenile.'

In her MG coupé we were bowling along a switchback Cotswold road towards her parents' country house. Her father had provided a suitable reason for her to 'go down' for the weekend. He was a valued friend of her college. 'What is the use of having money,' she had observed, 'if you don't use it to get what you want?'

The house would be empty except for the servants. Her father was at their London house, her mother wintering in Nice, and her younger sister at school in Switzerland.

This was my first car journey. I was glad it was in the dark, the sense of magic, of freedom, of taking wing, heightened. She handled the sprightly car with relaxed skill, her exhilaration overflowing and possessing me too. We spoke little. Communion was emphasised, not broken, by thoughts that bubbled to the surface.

The early winter sunset had left behind a sky of hard grey steel. In a scattering of high cirrus the stars gleamed sullenly. Hills were dark shapes against the sky, dark against dark. We were alone on the clear road, the very infrequent oncoming vehicle visible miles ahead. Like a racing driver on a track she took a line straight through curves, and cornered by hugging the outer lip till she could aim the car to slice off the arc and resume her direct line on the other end of it, the bodywork swinging outwards at the turn as if it tried to leave the wheels to their tighter course, and yawing inwards again as we re-entered the straight, throwing us together in the cramped cabin, joined in breath and body. The only illumination came from our dipped lights reflected from the cambered road sliding towards us beneath the bonnet, and gleaming dully on bare brown hedges moving steadily past, and from two little green bulbs on the dashboard. Their eerie luminescence picked out in soft chiaroscuro her finely rounded classical features, gleams in the curls cascading to her shoulders, tiny glints in her great eyes – Aphrodite in tender meditation, sailing through the night.

'What's wrong with them?' I asked.

I envied them for their sophistication, their poise, their worldly competence. They had accounts with tailors and bookmakers, drove cars,
sailed yachts to the Baltic, flew planes, were much travelled, moved with
ease in society. In this view of them I was being juvenile too; and I would
blush in retrospect. Whether she noted this at the time – or had already
sensed it and in her love forgiven it – I would never know.

The road reared up again and she changed down with a burst of engine
revolutions – a racing change, she called it, that Geoffrey Fiorenza had
taught her.

She murmured peevishly: 'They are so wrapped up in their pretty
selves. They haven't a notion how to treat a woman.'

At the crest of the hill she moved briskly into top gear and flicked on
the overdrive switch.

'They are so . . .' She searched for the word, gave up, and rushed on.
'What do you think of this? I went to Geoffrey's rooms for tea and he
showed me photos of racing cars till I wanted to scream! I popped into
his bedroom and slipped my knickers off and came back and said I
wanted to do a cartwheel. His sitting room's quite big, you know. Before
he could answer I did one, and then I stood in front of him and asked
him if he'd seen my ace of spades! You'll never guess what he did. He
said, "Careful! You might break some of the Sèvres," and turned back
to his blessed photograph album.'

I saw the flying thighs and the upturned skirt hem descending, and my
flesh grew hot; and then, green as I was, there came a prudish reaction.
A Gorbals girl would not have expressed her pique in that outrageous
fashion. She would have broken off with the man, 'respectably', and
taken care to be seen with him no more. Rachel's set, smart, glossy,
arrogant, was hard, and in its way cruel; it had little forbearance with the
weak or the unsure. Beneath her abrasive impatience, however, there
must surely be some sensitivity, some tenderness? As if answering me, I
sensed within her another, gentler, sentiment, almost an appeal:

> 'Oh God where shall I find
> A soul to listen,
> Not to words but to my heart,
> And speak to my condition?'

49

I wanted that too – I always had. I had thought I had found that soul in Annie – my first love, alas indelible – and how wrong I had been. Annie's desertion of me, for money, or the hope of it, had taught me something of worldliness. On that view, money was the key to everything, to choice, to the shaping of life. Rachel possessed that key. She could have virtually anything she wanted, *do* anything she wished with her life. Why, then, such savage discontent? I knew the answer. We both knew it – she from riches and I from poverty – and, with our differing prejudices, we fought against the knowledge. Annie was wrong: goods only got you part of the way, the rest was inside you. I had already set it out in the scholarship essay, but with the mind only, not in the language of the heart.

'What are you thinking about?' she asked.

Later, too late – oh that repeated story! – I would see how much I had underrated her, the sensibility, the courage. The reason she had told me of that incident in Fiorenza's rooms had almost passed me by. It was obvious enough – a contrast in sensibility. She saw in me, rightly or wrongly, a light that drew her – we saw it in each other:

'Think each in each, immediately wise . . .'

Did I really possess such riches? I wanted to believe it.

'I was thinking about money,' I said, surprising myself. 'And whether one can be happy without it.' Then added, hastily, 'How stupid that sounds!'

'I wonder about it too. I feel one *should* be able to. But you said something a moment ago, so quietly all I heard was '. . . speak to my condition.'

I said the lines again. She repeated them and was silent. Then she said in a whisper: 'Never to explain – ask or be asked? How beautiful life would be – how free?'

It was too much to ask of life. Some part of you must be kept inviolate. With Annie I had given without reserve, and she had inflicted a wound that would never heal. And so, in fear, you invented excuses to avoid handing yourself over so completely ever again – myths and superstitions so transparent you were half ashamed of them, but potent none the less. 'Was love,' Bernard once asked, 'like beauty, no more than a dream in the soul of the beholder?' Love was an indulgence. Tread that path with care. In the commerce of the heart, as in so much else, I was ill-equipped to deal as an equal with these gilded people, endowed as they were with unquenchable confidence, schooled to *expect* success in whatever they touched. And always, in the last resort, they had money to cushion a fall. Part of me knew that this was callow stuff. Sooner or later the heart would win, and throw me into the mêlée to take my chance.

Echoing my thoughts she murmured: 'One has to trust – sooner or later. There's no choice.'

We went through a village strung out along a single wide street, most of it in darkness or deep shadow, except for a cone of weak gaslight from a street lamp near each end, scattered glimmers from curtained cottage windows and, near the middle, a patch of intense yellow light from two oil-burning carriage lamps hanging from iron brackets on the doorposts of a half-timbered inn. A group of men, their trousers corded at the knees, leaned on bicycles and talked.

A mile or so beyond the village we slowed at a break in the grass verge, turned into it and rolled to a stop, facing ornate iron park gates flanked by massive cylindrical gateposts of rusticated stone. A few yards within, the lighted windows of a stone lodge shone warmly in the surrounding blackness. Someone within must have been watching for us, for hardly had Rachel drawn the handbrake lever up on its ratchet than the door opened and the black silhouette of a stocky man in gaiters appeared in the rectangle of yellow light. The man hurried towards the gates and heaved them open.

Wheels crunching and crackling on the gravel of a tree-lined estate road, we drove round the base of some rising ground for about a quarter of a mile; then the main headlights picked out a Palladian façade, with broad steps leading up to a portico above a sunken ground floor.

She left the engine running, and we mounted the steps and went through the wide front door. From behind us there floated up, in the crisp notes of night, the sounds of the car boot being opened and our bags lifted out, then the wheels rustling on the gravel once again as the car was driven round to the back of the house. She led the way up a broad wooden staircase that rose from the middle of a square entrance hall lined with dark linenfold panelling, along a corridor hung with William Morris paper – large panels of pastel blue foliage on a primrose ground. She half-opened a door and paused, hand on the doorknob.

I glimpsed a four-poster bed from whose canopy hung silk curtains embroidered with tea roses. Silently, by the way she stood, the slight inclination of the head, an expression at once audacious and wary, she warned me that people were listening, watching. Though our purpose in the house must be perfectly obvious to the staff, we must follow a code. She nodded towards a door opposite hers: 'They'll put your bag in that guest room.'

Keeping straight faces we managed a smile of complicity, and turned away to our separate rooms. I took off my stiff fustian overcoat and dropped it on the settle at the foot of the bed, a narrower version of the one in her room. Our Gorbals flat could have been put into this room with space to spare. This was luxury I had seen only in films. The cream rugs on the polished wooden floor seemed ankle deep. Before a broad-paned window stood a curved dressing table draped in the same heavy silk that curtained the bed, on it a looking-glass triptych framed in gold. Beside a second window was a gilt writing table with slender fluted legs, covered in gold-tooled calf. Opposite the bed was a door; the room had its very own bathroom, with toilet *and* a bidet. Here was a life and a half.

The butler, white haired, had the compact figure and economy of movement that often indicates the neatness and precision learned in the Navy; gravely he served dinner, assisted by a pretty dark-haired girl of about sixteen in crisp white apron and frilled cap. I sat with Rachel at the end of a long mahogany table, beneath a chandelier whose crystal pendants cast rainbow gleams on silver and stiff white linen. A log fire crackled in a tall fireplace of green marble, a high brass fender before it. We talked little, our silences close.

She said softly: 'I am not a bit promiscuous. No, that's not what I meant to say. I mean this. If we . . .' She sighed, then words came with a rush: 'I think I want to live with you.'

I was dismally provincial, for the words startled me. Intellectually, safely in the abstract, one was expected to show sympathy with the raffish goings-on of the smart set; you took part eagerly in coffee-table chatter about trial marriage, a modish theme among progressive women under-graduates. It all seemed so mature, so adventurous, but it was surely not 'me'. It was not, in the deeply incised Gorbals judgment, 'respectable'. Here it was, however, close beside me, not abstract but real, her dark-scented flesh breathing it and speaking it – romantic, and yet daunting. Shocking thoughts crowded in. The kind of behaviour that people of her set looked upon with jaded eye, in the Gorbals was anathema – though it happened!

Was there not a rule in the boss class: 'Never comment on a likeness'? Immorality such as ours was to be this very night – here under a parental roof – would be unthinkable in the Gorbals, where lovers were expected to stand together at the rubbish heap at the back of the close. In the boss class, money shut people's mouths, made certain actions invisible, and many things smell sweeter than they were. Above all you sinned in comfort, in style – and in a fashion respectably.

But living together? In the Gorbals morality, Jewish influences were joined with the host culture – Calvinist fundamentalism linked to Dickensian calculation. The latter now pulled me up short. A girl's value in the marriage market was sharply diminished by a 'previous canter over the course', as the sardonic vernacular put it. For that reason if for no other she would – she *must* –cling to you, literally for dear life. And worse still, if she was 'knocked up', be she ever so smart and modern, all the fine talk of *trial* marriage would fly straight out of the window! In pure self-interest would she ever let you go free?

How lovely she was! In the light of the leaping flames she glowed from within like a goddess. She had come down to dinner in a clinging dress of black velvet. A rope of pearls was just long enough to hang below the curved décolletage. Now and then the lowest pearls slipped behind and were gripped between her breasts, and she freed them with a lift of the shoulders and flick of a forefinger in the cleavage. How heady to be here at her right hand, her consort in this her palace, and hear her say, confidently, with longing, words of blessing and joy and accolade: 'I want to live with you.'

Prosaic thoughts, churlish, selfish, intervened again – ashes in the mouth. Living together would entail abandoning Oxford. For one of her class that would be unimportant. For me, having reached Oxford by a million-to-one chance, how could I throw it all overboard now! There would be no other way; it would be impossible to support a woman on my scholarship money; I would have to get a job. And what was I fitted for? Only the pressing? How could I take a girl like her back to all that? Simplistic Gorbals verities asserted themselves, man the

---

53

breadwinner, woman the homemaker. Doubtless that was why, in retrospect hard to believe, the idea that we might live on *her* money did not immediately occur to me. That would mean, despicably, being a kept man! Even if I did somehow stretch my scholarship stipend to support us both, what about the future, when I went down? So far, I had sailed along totally absorbed in books and lectures and friendship and talk, discovery and self-discovery – a marvellous licence, with no thought for a tomorrow that remained invisible beyond the horizon. When that final day did come, I would be back, literally without a penny, where I had started.

As if she had listened to my thoughts she broke in, spitting out the words in a fierce whisper: 'Don't – please – think about *money*. Money's irrelevant.' She raged at the world.

We left the dining-room and crossed the hall, shadowy now, lit from wall lamps at the top of the monumental wooden staircase, and by a gleam from the logs in the room we had left. The house was sinking into the night, the only sounds the muted voices and clatter of dishes and pots drifting up from the floor below. We went into a small room on the other side of the staircase, furnished in glowing mahogany, with heavy tapestry curtains. A brass standard lamp, silk shade depicting flamingoes feeding, stood in each corner. On a small sideboard near the door were two silver trays, one with decanters of whisky, brandy and sherry, and assorted glasses, and another with a glass coffee percolator on its diminutive spirit stove, tiny cups and saucers, cream jug and sugar bowl of fluted silver. We sat close together on a long leather sofa facing a fire whose logs gave off an unfamiliar scent, a mixture of resin and pine and lavender.

'There is so little time,' she murmured, 'almost no time at all.' She leaned her head on my shoulder. Despite the room's warmth, she shivered. 'There's something I must show you tomorrow.'

She added hurriedly: 'No, don't ask me now. It's – it's a sign of where we all are in the world.'

She got up and absently smoothed the dress over her hips and went to the little sideboard. She refilled our cups, half-turned and said timidly: 'I don't really drink. I feel like it tonight, though.'

I awoke, as I thought, within a dream. I was in the curtained alcove bed in our Gorbals kitchen, in the days when as a little child I shared it with father and mother. In a half-light full of shadows, the curtains were closing in on me, brushing my face. I turned my head to look out through a chink where two edges barely met, aware of the silvery shimmer of a winter dawn, expecting to see the rough kitchen table with its cracked oilcloth cover, and beyond it the shallow earthenware sink, and above it the grimy window panes dimly showing the dark slate roofs of the tenement on the other side of Warwick Street. Instead, I saw a dressing table hung with close-pleated flowered silk down to the deep pile ivory carpet, with an array of silver-topped bottles on it, and beyond, through large window panes – clear but bearing the ghostly mark of the night's frost – a fairy tracery of branches picked out in white rime, just beginning to be touched by the delicate watercolour pink of the awakening sun. Rachel stirred beside me, shifted closer so that her face fitted into the hollow of my shoulder, murmured something, and slept on.

And so I lay in this magic bed of silk, pauper into prince, suspended in wonder, her breathing the distant suspiration of waves heard in a sea shell, her breast gently rising on my ribs and softly subsiding, a caress lovingly repeated; a still moment between two fragments of time, of revelation, of awareness. Life was taking yet another great leap into the unknown, as on the day, a century ago, when I ripped open that first letter from Oxford, or in the gleams of new certainty that came and went in this new life.

For the very first time it seemed, I tried to look emotion in the face – how juvenile that sounds – and yet it was probably true. Desire and sentiment had always masqueraded as one and the same. Now, sated from the night, I could attempt to see them apart. Love, happiness, commitment, attachment – where was their place in the ebb and flow of lust?

'The natural vigour in the venial sin . . .'

And where did calculation – the enemy of love I had always thought – have its place, as it seemed to have in other people? Here I was, so close to Rachel that her flesh was part of me, how could I think of her – of us – so coolly? Alec had said I must learn to be callous; was this what he meant? I was detached as I had never been with Annie, and that *must* be wrong. Love alone should be real – the world an enigmatic mirage.

What alchemy of the soul had taken me back to that kitchen bed –

where mother had died – to re-affirm the indelible stamp of that other life? What *was* this message from the Kindly Ones?

I recalled another dawn long ago, when I had awakened with Annie in that broken Roman embrasure on Carbeth Muir, a silken moment too. Then I thought of the moment on the factory steps when she told me we were finished – in effect, that my 'prospects' were not good enough. I waited for the wound to hurt freshly once more, as it had done unfailingly before. Instead the vision receded, lost its sharpness. The pain was no more than a contrived memory. The time would come when even that would slide away and only mourning remain, to be transmuted in the end into simple regret.

And what of this, joined with her, flesh breathing with flesh in this silk-curtained bed – would this exaltation fall away in its turn? And others, each in a fashion also incomplete, follow after?

About a hundred yards from the house, at the base of the hillock we had skirted when we arrived, we entered a copse, the path twisting through shrubbery and spreading oaks. Rachel stepped confidently ahead, and soon we stood before an old stone doorway set into the rising turf, flanked by Doric columns supporting a classical pediment. We entered a bunker equipped as a last refuge from the irresistible devastation from the air that was talked about in the press as the dominant feature of the next war – the bomber would always get through – no place in town or country would be immune. Here were rooms with desks and typewriters, telephones and teleprinters; there were Spartan sleeping quarters, food stores, water from an underground spring, fuel supplies, a generator.

She said: 'Papa's main business will move down to the house when war comes. But he's hoping that if air raids don't get here too often the staff can work mostly *above* ground. The old stables at the back are being got ready for that. They'll live in the house and in cottages round about.'

The room was cold and still as a tomb. Beneath the harsh neon light, its infernal hues relentlessly flickering, her features were drained of colour; or was the cause within her? Forlornly she looked about, her lips moving as if she whispered a prayer. Perhaps a benign spirit, guardian of the earth that pressed down upon us here, would pronounce a reassuring spell?

Feverishly her words tumbled out: 'I don't *want* to believe this. You saw those black boxes – fireproof storage for the records papa's had photographed and brought down. That shows you where we really *are*? What's the use of dreaming any more? What future is there to plan for? Oh God in heaven, there *is* no time left. No time at all.'

The place was awesome in its cold stillness, its sense of anticipation, its readiness for the last trump. There was nothing new in the message, only that there was no further retreat. Here under a green hill in the heart of England, in a meticulously planned business fortress waiting to outface the collapse of the known world, pretence crumpled. The savage promise of the times would *not* pass us by, or mercifully strike others instead.

'Let us be happy in each other,' she murmured. 'Let us imagine that time stands still. We might only have days, weeks, a few months at the most. What is there to lose? Nothing. Oxford? My God, at a time like this how can you even think about that?'

On the face of it she was right. But it was easy for her. For children of the boss class, Oxford was nothing more than a playtime interval, a place, or rather a state of mind, in which to drift in pleasurable experiment – a shadow play till you made up your mind to face the real world. For me? Were there any words to explain it? – a pilgrim's progress, though to what salvation I had no idea.

She raged at me, but tenderly. 'That's all for nothing *now*! Don't you see? And for heaven's sake don't worry about money. You're clever, you'll get a job. Papa will help when he's faced with it. Anyway, I've got money of my own. Dearest, there's so little time!'

Ah yes – to be a *kept man*? The respectability principle of the Gorbals, honoured even while necessity enforced its betrayal, stared at me piti-lessly. Many men in the Gorbals, in bad times, had been just that; but no one dared criticise, for who knew where hardship would strike next? But in her class, being a kept man seemed neither uncommon nor particularly noteworthy; respectability was liberally interpreted; you did what you wanted to do – and your money *made* the rules fit.

Mean thoughts returned. What if the world did *not* crumble around us, and our idyll, confronting 'the long littleness of life', faded into nothing? Would *she* suffer as I would? Of course not; she would simply go back to papa and take up the pampered life as before. And

I? What would I do, left stranded – in some ways worse off than before?

I was humbled by these thoughts. I fancy she sensed them. There was no reproach, only sympathy, a kind of support. To *understand* was beyond her.

And so the insistent dialogue of lovers continued. Walking in the woods in the chill March air, or gazing into the log fire in the little sitting-room, and later, back in Oxford on the windy towpath, we fought for answers – except that the fight was one-sided; for her there was simply the decision to be made and let the future look after itself, what was left of it. As for me, I fought with fear itself, without faith.

Marriage, of course, was not considered. After all, there was no need to, this was to be a trial marriage! It was *the* daring adventure. She mentioned marriage only in passing, as a distant possibility – 'something we could grow into'.

Again and again she wrestled with my financial fears, to her incomprehensible. One day she said: 'Listen, I am of age. I suppose I could settle something on you. I mean, to make you feel less dependent on me – and maybe to cope with emergencies? If it would make you feel better, I could get the lawyers to put it in some sort of trust?'

She said it from a good heart, but in sadness. Why could I not say, as she did, let's seize fulfilment while we can, and to hell with everything?

7

Philip Toynbee:
the Soul-Mate Treatment

In spells of remission we would be happy for a few days; then lightning would strike once more, as likely as not from a clear sky.

On a blustery March afternoon we were on the river path leading to the Trout Inn at Godstow, a popular walk when work lay in the doldrums between lunch and tea. Strung out on the windy bank, dozens of couples walked close, or strode with hands linked and arms outstretched in confiding separation – exulting in love's conquest of the world. In warmer weather some might leave the path and wander to the far side of one of the fields that stretched away from the river; and there under a hedge, or the sand-coloured cobbled wall of ruined Godstow Abbey further along near the Trout, they would primly sit and commune.

We, too, floated along in our private world. Suddenly she broke the silence as if a dormant pain had burst into wakefulness and must be transferred at once. She struck at Werner, or appeared to; if it had not been for him, she said, 'I would never have got to know you at all.'

That, she implied, would have saved her much heartache.

I almost welcomed the chill bite of the wind that cut the face with the fine sting of a razor blade. It drove the steel grey water beside us into angry white-edged wavelets, with a crisp rustling sound like tearing paper. Beyond the river, on the distant edge of the empty steppe of Port Meadow, the sad poplars leaned down low. Was our case hopeless? Were our tempers so opposed that all effort at fusion must fail? If our coming together had been one of Destiny's false throws, perhaps our felicity was false too, not worth fighting to preserve? Or was this the denouement Werner had warned me against: 'These *Hofjuden* can take you up, simply to satisfy their curiosity, and drop you – hard.'

I wanted to banish defeat from her mind. I told her of the day when I had seen her riding down the Broad with the others, in passion hurling

'Hatikvah' at the Trinity window where the swastika flag hung; and Werner, seeing I wanted her, brought us together.

The sun broke through in her again. She shook her hair in the wind, and murmured: 'Do you believe in Destiny?'

Oh that poignant question, asked all around us!

'We have to. For that matter, what brought Werner here?'

That might not be a happy way to put it, linking our happiness with that disaster for our people – for the world – which had brought Werner here. I had assumed that she knew he had been in Buchenwald. Amazingly she did not. On an impulse I decided to enlist sympathy for him. After all these months he was still waiting for the committee to decide whether he was to receive the research appointment. Werner was deeply European; to stay and work in England was important to him, a toehold in the culture. And now, giving up hope, he was making plans to join his family in America. Would her father intercede with the committee?

I did not understand that my impulse could be suspect, the selfish temptation to shift the course of someone else's life. I had still to learn that the Fates, in their refined irony, transmuted good intentions into the tragic, the grotesque.

She was moved, but I saw a shadow of something else, perhaps the guilt that fleetingly haunts the fortunate at such a moment.

Usually so quick, she did not reply at once, but walked on with head bent; then, speaking somewhat woodenly as if overcoming reservations, she said: 'All right. I'll speak to papa.'

She implied that her father would do what she asked. But the hesitation worried me.

She looked ahead along the path, eyes half-closed to the wind. Her manner changed suddenly, as if a blind was lifted, and her usual social gleam, the facile surface gloss, shone out. Coming towards us from the direction of Godstow was a tight little group, happily noisy, overflowing the narrow path on to the sparse grass at the side. Six girls, hair and scarves blowing, jostled round the tall saturnine figure of Philip Toynbee, in thick tweed jacket and flannels, dark hair standing on end in the wind, head intently inclined.

We were on the last stretch of the meandering path before Godstow, the Trout Inn a few hundred yards ahead on its spit of land beside the high arched bridge, and in front of it the weir, gate-like, that brought to mind the bridge on a willow-pattern plate, standing high and solitary in the swirling waters. A wooden farm gate stretched across the path before us, with a swinging wicket at its side nearest the water. Here part of the bank had fallen away taking a slice of the path with it, leaving a narrow ledge of wet and slippery earth that one crossed by gripping the post on which the wicket gate swung and taking a great step, almost a leap, across. The manoeuvre needed care, for with the collapse of the path the gate-post was unsteady in its few remaining inches of muddy earth at the water's edge. Philip and his companions came up as we passed through. Recognising me, his heavy features assumed the familiar rallying scrutiny, with just the hint of a smile – the commissar showing humanity. Perhaps to impress his girls, and possibly Rachel too, he launched into the aggressive banter then fashionable, whose aim was to 'wrong-foot' you into taking up an untenable position – in this instance political.

Philip could redeem a patrician flintiness with a convincing warmth and a highly developed sense of humour. When I had parried a few thrusts, he shook his head ruefully, more concerned not to lose face with the girls than with the substance, such as it was, of our exchange. 'Look,' he said, 'let's be serious. The proletariat is by nature politically conscious, and we've got to accept our responsibility in the fight against the fascists. If you don't come in now you'll be numbered among the class enemy when the time comes.'

'Did you say *we*? And *our* responsibility? Come off it, Philip, since when have *you* numbered yourself among the proletariat?'

Unusually for him, he was momentarily at a loss. 'If only,' his expression seemed to say, 'I could *be* a proletarian for one moment, just to prove I mean all I say – the one attribute I lack?'

One of the girls, who wore heavy gold earrings in the form of the hammer and sickle, giggled at the notion of the proletarian Toynbee, then saw that she had struck a wrong note and hastily tried another: 'Oh Philip do let's hurry. The crumpets and anchovy toast will be gone if we linger.'

Recovering, he looked at her in exaggerated horror: 'We mustn't miss that at any price, must we?'

He stood aside for them to stream past, and watched each girl point a foot and skip across the watery gap in the path and let the gate swing back for the next to follow. When they had all gone through he turned to me. 'All right, *touché*. But the point is this. We've entered a period of wars and revolutions – that's the Comintern analysis – and the logical place for a chap like you is in the Party. You've got a historic role in all this don't forget. You and I must have a serious talk. I'm in Beaumont Street you know – do come in and see me. I must go now.'

Years later I would stand at that spot and see stretched before me along the path a straggling column of phantoms, weary *revenants* haunting their past. Each in a fashion had faced the world heroically, and ardently striven to place a healing hand upon the future, and found that nothing of importance consented to be changed. I would see how truly, but with what poignantly twisted meaning, the words 'historic role' fitted them. That exchange with Philip, so symptomatic of the time, would return charged with its earnestness, its fervent but insecure hope, and in a mysterious way ritualistic, as if we had uttered words written for us long before. It was hard to believe that anyone could have thought in Byronic images at such a time. We did feel that we were about to play roles in a world tragedy, the greatest ever known, but at the same time, confusedly, obstinately, even though we suspected that our entrances and exits were already written, we insisted that we could stand against the Fates and force them to yield – in *some* things at least – when the trumpets sounded.

When Philip and his party had gone, and we were plodding along the muddy path to the Trout, Rachel sniffed: 'How *dare* he hector you like that? Serious talk indeed!'

Philip had gone down about a year before, but he was still much in evidence. He had enjoyed power through the Party, and the thrill of continuing to do so, through friends still up as well as in his own right – apart from continuing a hectic emotional life – drew him back.

An especially magnetic facet of that power, where a party mandarin was at the centre of a spider's web of manipulation, was control of the 'marking' – covert cultivation – of students thought worth 'bringing in' as Party jargon had it, as into a sacred community of the elect. A Party member, chosen for compatibility with an intended recruit – the target – would be ordered to make his acquaintance and try to become friends with him. The target would not know that he had been chosen. The 'marker' would pretend that the relationship was one of soul-mates, an idea that had a powerful appeal in a generation for which Pater's hard gemlike flame still held enchantment. Progress would be reported to a special committee, which would guide the marker through the changing subtleties of the Party line, and tell him how to overcome emotional or intellectual stumbling blocks. The Party leader, or one of the leadership group – sometimes called the Peckwater Gang because several of its members had rooms in the Christ Church quad of that name – would decide when the marker should reveal that he was a Party member; and, later, when the moment was ripe to invite the target – often with a baleful emotional ultimatum – to 'come in'.

If the marking had been skilful, an appeal to the target's sense of historic purpose, dizzyingly attractive to the romantic spirit in that tense time, could usually be relied upon to sweep away remaining doubts. Post-war revelations about the Cambridge traitors suggest, not surprisingly, that a similar soul-mate method was used to recruit them.

If the ultimatum failed, the target would be invited to a 'serious talk' with a leading member of the Party. Often this would be Philip, who enjoyed the role of spiritual guide; perhaps it helped to allay his own hunger for certainty.

The words 'a serious talk', with their overtones of familial concern, the strong hand of support on the shoulder, were intentionally misleading; they were code for 'We will *make* you see the light.' Sensing this, a nervous undergraduate worried about the state of his soul could find the prospect alarming as he made his way to Peckwater, blind to the grace of the facade, finding its patrician seclusion menacing, to face a Party mandarin, fluent and steely, sitting behind a green-baize table like an examining magistrate.

Philip gloried in personifying the Party's ethos of paternalism and menace. If, when the time came, it was in the Party's interest to send someone to the firing squad, he said, he would do so without hesitation. In him there was an irreconcilable conflict between the dreamer with his shifting visions of the quest for utopia, and the man of action hungry for simplistic belief on which the trumpets could confidently ring and the banners fly. Hence the attraction of Marxism's seeming elegance and symmetry. Being a revolutionary, for his upper-class coterie of the far left, was an élitist game in which, as when playing soldiers in the nursery, *they* must naturally be the commanders; and with total assurance they took it for granted that after the revolution the top places would again be theirs. It was an assumption that made them more ruthless than many true proletarians.

To be fair, Philip had more sensitivity than many of them. That attribute, allied to a questioning tendency that Party discipline only temporarily held in check, would in the years to come lead him away from its narrow absolutism. Then, in sadness and some confusion, he would seek in vain a substitute for the old certainty – in founding a commune, for example – with which to regain the lost glory of spiritual leader.

In those passionate Oxford days, his could be a refreshing spirit. He could make you feel that in the next moment, with the very next word, you might change the world. He had come close to it in our exchange on the river path. We must cry '*no pasaran!*' to the fascists all over again. We must choose between nemesis if we sided with the forces of evil – in effect if we did nothing – and retribution from the Party when, after victory at the barricades, power was in its hands. That was not really a choice at all, a confusion that was not typical of him. Perhaps he had been distracted by the adoration of his band of admirers, but that too was unlike him. Franco *had* passed. Mussolini and Hitler *were* going from strength to strength. In country after country the Leninist 'revolutionary situation' which the party must bring about and then manipulate to obtain power – in Spain, Czechoslovakia, Greece – had been a mirage.

Rachel said, 'Philip is quite sweet in a *louche* sort of way. One simply can't *believe* he's as ruthless as he pretends.'

At the Trout we stood for a few minutes on the stone steps at the end of its promontory, the river at our feet noisy as a millrace. A short distance off, in a twelve-foot dinghy stopped near a submerged tree root, was Bill Challoner, another Party mandarin, son of a rich landowning house. I had recently taught myself to sail such a craft, renting it at the sailing club, and the thrill of the wind's power, the pulse of the elements felt in the vibrations of the sheet, was a spiritual revelation like the one on the tennis court. In our progress along the path I had watched him reaching smoothly up the river, and wondered idly how he would manage the return trip. Sailing up river on this stretch, the wind was usually astern, and took you here more or less on a straight course; but to get back down river demanded an athletic tacking back and forth hard into the wind, and you made distance in short zig-zags across the narrow channel.

Bill had brought the boat up with a fierce slapping of the sail. Now he braced himself across the stern seat and went about, and with a thwack the little sail filled, and he took the boat across, wavelets rapping on the timbers, to within a few feet of the opposite bank. He came up with what must have been only inches of depth to spare, went about smartly and tacked and sailed back again – and so, back and forth, shifting his weight from one side of the little boat to the other in precise timing for the turn, he went swinging away down river.

In our separate silences we turned away from the noisy rush of the waters and went into the Inn. The low-beamed parlour, hung with clammy river air, felt grey and cold. In the wide stone hearth a pile of resinous logs crackled and spat, and smoky flames rose, fell back, rose again, trying hard to dry the air. I went to the tap room window and ordered tea and hot crumpets. Rachel stood on the hearth stone and shook her hair loose, but did not stretch her hands to the fire, though her knuckles had been chilled blue through the red woollen mittens. There was a new, indefinable tension in her.

Dully she said, not looking at me, 'I'll get papa on the phone.'

In a mysterious association of ideas, as I stood contemplating the smoky flames, I had a vision of Alec, earthy, stoical, at his place at the other side of the pressing-table. What would he think of my life here – sailing on the river, the exchanges with Philip, Rachel immeasurable distances removed from Annie or Bunty, my stumbling efforts to unlock the codes of this place?

She returned and joined me on the hearth. Her father had been shocked to hear that the committee had kept the distinguished scientist waiting so long. He would speak to the chairman.

'Werner will get his appointment.'

She stood only inches away from the fire, and shivered. 'You wondered why I hesitated to speak to papa? Werner doesn't seem to be pining for his wife, does he? That's why. Never mind. I've done it for *you*.' She spoke with unfamiliar gloom, with a kind of resignation.

The change was baffling. Sophisticated, tough in a fashion, was she reverting to an ancestral type? I had a vision of mother from long ago, and heard her tired tones when father had come home skint and she must rush out to the pawnshop to rescue him. It was not a parallel at all, but in feeling it was close enough. Why had I been so insensitive?

––––––

In getting her father to intercede for Werner had she really gone against her principles? Or was this seeming resurgence of Mrs Grundy simply a woman's 'fancy idea', as Alec might have called it, a tactic in manipulation? With thoughts of permanence with *me*, did she hope to place contamination as far away as possible? Werner's infidelities, she was saying, cancelled his sufferings. He deserved no help, no sympathy.

Like everyone else around us she had always talked flippantly about morals. I had failed to sense the conventional prejudices strongly in place beneath. And now they had surfaced as feminine solidarity with a wronged woman.

How could I have foreseen all this? Yet I should have done. I had no excuse. I needed to find so many answers! Where, with whom, would I find them?

For the first time since I had left the Gorbals I longed for the pace of experience to slow down.

'Farfalla in tempesta,
Under rain in the night . . .'

I thought of *L'Education Sentimentale*. When would mine truly begin? I was a greenhorn, stumbling, falling, where others floated so confidently. Would I ever draw level with them?

A week or so later, Werner was bubbling over with his news. 'Can you believe it? I had just got my passage confirmed, and now the committee have written to say I have the appointment! And so now I must go into reverse and get my wife and children over here, which should not be hard because most people are going in the opposite direction! God knows if this is the right thing I'm doing.'

Fearfully, without knowing why, I echoed the question.

The day would come when I would curse myself for a blundering busybody. Time and events would have shifted, and perspectives with them, their significance hidden, but in retrospect painfully predictable. Waiting lists for Atlantic passages would lengthen. By the time Werner's wife and children embarked for Britain, war would have come. Werner would be interned in the Isle of Man as an enemy alien, and for that he cursed the whole world; how could they do that to *him*, a persecuted Jew from Buchenwald? While there, his wife and children would be killed in one of the early German hit-and-run raids. Shortly afterwards he would be released and return to Oxford for secret war work – but still, as he put it with a spark of his old irony, 'with them but not *of* them; the eternal fate of the Jew.'

I never dared tell him that I had meddled in his destiny – with goodwill as I had thought at the time, but in truth arrogantly. I should have consulted him first. Others had been punished in my stead, and their fate would haunt me in nightmares of blood.

Perhaps, after all, Rachel *had* been right? Someone must always suffer. Perhaps Werner was punished, if that was the right word, justly? These questions would never be answered. I would never silence the guilt. The sure touch that others possessed – as I thought – and which I so envied, would remain tantalisingly out of reach.

Ashenden's World

I was never given the soul-mate treatment. But I cannot be sure. The Byzantine world of the Party was the one bit of Oxford life in which I thought I knew my way. Bernard had illuminated the Party's ways for me, but there was much he had left obscure, perhaps in self-preservation, especially the indistinct area where agitprop shaded away into secret work. The Party's intelligence was good. When I first set foot in Oxford the mandarins were aware of my links with the renegade Bernard; they must have concluded that in some respects I knew too much. Their approach was therefore more direct, invitations to front organisation meetings for Spanish refugees, to join study groups on Fascism – but never, significantly, any effort to oppose Mosley's anti-semitism. Now and then one of the mandarins buttonholed me. Why didn't I come in? With my proletarian background, was I not better equipped for a leading role than even some of them might be?

One encounter, seemingly without a hint of politics, took a course that in wildest fantasy I would never have foreseen.

Bill Challoner was tall and slender, with sharp features, lank fair hair drooping over a high forehead, and deep blue watchful eyes. He was neither the demagogue nor the Marxist theoretician; indeed he appeared to have no interest in doctrine. Quiet-spoken, attentive, courteous, a person of long tranquil silences, of the apt word at the chosen moment, his forte was deceptive charm. From one of the older public schools he had come up to read modern languages, and was in his final year; he intended to follow an older brother into the foreign service. Would his Party card be an obstacle there, I once asked him. He found the question amusing: 'Of course not! The family's connections are quite sound.'

I met him occasionally at the sailing club, where I regularly took out a dinghy for a shilling. One day, when I was at the little wooden office at the moorings about to book a boat, he sauntered up. He was taking out his brand new fourteen-foot International for the first time – would

I care to join him? I had never sailed this big-canvassed dinghy, designed for racing; indeed it was odd to see one here at all, for it was too fast for this narrow piece of Oxford water. Still, the invitation was a compliment; club members must have noted my fledgling ability with approval.

We strolled along the gently swaying raft beneath the leaning trees to its far end nearest the channel, and there the slim brown boat gleamed in the slanting sun of the waning day, the roped-down canvas glossy with newness. Bill stood aside to let me be first aboard; a little breathless I stepped on to the untrodden duckboard and felt the adhesion of new varnish under foot.

There was a momentary stab of envy. To buy this new boat and indulge a whim, Bill had spent more than I ever earned in the factory in a whole year.

We raised sail, the new cordage running grittily in spite of its wax, and shoved off from the raft. We swayed and drifted slowly in the brown shallows dappled with long splashes of sun low in a sky streaked with lavender. The mainsail flapped stiffly, then seemed to draw to itself the gently moving air and half-filled; the sleek shell rocked uncertainly, hesitated, went ahead and stayed and went ahead again, then, as the canvas caught a stronger surge of air, moved confidently forward with a knock and chuckle of water, as if the craft were talking to the wind and the river. Away from the sheltering trees we skimmed over ripples dancing with gold. Dun-coloured banks and meadows of sombre winter green drifted by; and so, dreaming, we were wafted up river. Near Godstow, seeing the lavender in the sky darkening to grey, we decided to start back immediately, for though the wind remained light, tacking in the narrow water, in an unfamiliar boat in full darkness, might bring us badly foul of the bank.

Remote from the world in the descending darkness, we set about tacking back and forth, alert to bring the sprightly craft up and about smartly, working together with precision, hardly speaking. We beat back with only a few gentle groundings, when we misjudged the boat's power and were too slow in bringing her up and round for the next in the long succession of acute zig-zags.

The sky had lost all light when we steered for the narrow channel where the moorings lay, close to the lines of pollarded willows, their knobbed heads drooping meditatively in the obscurity. The night breeze freshening, we took in the mainsail, and with slackened jib she had enough way to bring us in steadily through ebony water flickering eerily with dulled reflections of distant lights. The line of masts at the moorings, ghostly in the darkness, slid into dim definition against gleams of paleness filtering between the trees. I took in the jib, and with our remaining way Bill brought her gently alongside the raft. We tied up, secured canvas and cordage and made all tidy and fast, retreating step by step, reluctantly, from the magical converse with the river.

Hungry, chilled by the clammy river air, we went back to his rooms for tea, talking little. Only as we neared his staircase did it occur to me that I had spent about two hours with a Party mandarin, and not a word of politics had been spoken. Then the spell of the river returned, and this passing curiosity faded.

His first-floor rooms, lofty, with floral plasterwork in white and gold in cornices and on walls, looked out over splendid lawns. We drew chintz-covered chairs close to the crackling coals in a tall fireplace of green marble. His scout, a tubby man in black alpaca jacket, with close-cropped white hair and the canny eyes of the old soldier, bustled in with a large brass-handled tray bearing a silver tea-pot, anchovy toast and fruit cake, the cups and saucers and plates embellished in gold leaf.

In the languid manner that suggested only a fleeting interest in the matter in hand, Bill mentioned an essay he had just written, on Goethe and the Romantic Movement. As it happened, I was intensely interested in the Romantics at this time, that explosion of creative thought so inadequately explained in reading and in lectures. We talked of French and German poetry. Surprisingly he knew that in addition to my main studies then – economics, political theory, philosophy, psychology – I had tutors in French and German. It was not difficult to discover what a student was reading, and with which tutor, but it would take a little trouble. Someone in the Party had gone to that trouble. Why? It might have been routine. Or perhaps it was a subtle, charming nicety on Bill's part, to find an interest we had in common, so that conversation might be free of politics?

My French tutor was the eccentric Mademoiselle Fleury, who dressed *comme matelot* in flared navy blue trousers, zephyr and rope sandals, always with a Caporal drooping from her lips, the first avowed lesbian I had ever met. I read German poetry with the aged, charming Fraulein

Wüschak, sometime governess in the Kaiser's family. Dressed in many layers of dusty velvet and gold brocade, she shared her Walton Street house with eighteen cats. Her manner, belying the cheery, rounded aspect of a good grandmother in a Grimms' fairy tale, was old-world and firm. If, struggling to say something in German, I took refuge in even a single word of English, she would not answer but prodded the air reprovingly with her cigarette in its long amber holder; I knew she would not relent – it was a matter of honour – until I conjured up enough German to fit. When I entered her dusty study, several cats squabbling fiercely about my ankles, she greeted me in the courtly fashion of a great lady in a gilded drawing room: 'Ah the young Herr Doctor!'; and I would think of the times when, as I stepped into the great arched reading room of the Mitchell Library in my ragged shorts or shabby working clothes, the staff murmured to one another 'Here comes the young professor.' Not much had changed.

With Mademoiselle Fleury that morning I had been struck by some lines in Ronsard's 'Sonnets pour Hèlàne', bittersweet, barbed, that drove home a feeling I had recognised and resisted long before, a sense of the intransigent flux of life, unappeasable in the midst of sweetness – intimations of mortality, of transient triumph. I tried out the thought on Bill:

> 'Quand vous serez bien vieille, au soir, à la chandelle,
> Assise auprês du feu, dévidant et filant,
> Direz, chantant mes vers, en vous émerveillant,
> Ronsard me célèbrait du temps que j'étais belle.'

He thought about it. 'It's too late then isn't it? Don't you feel that the blunt sentiments of "Gather ye rosebuds while ye may" are much nearer the mark?'

He started and looked at his wrist-watch, and almost in a single movement jumped to his feet, seized some papers from his desk, and was at the door: 'My God, I should be reading my essay this very minute! My dear chap, I do apologise. You *must* stay and finish the toast and so on, won't you?'

The door slammed. A moment later it swung open and he put his head round. 'A friend of my brother's may pop in. Interesting chap. Bit of a globe trotter. Make my apologies to him, will you? Oh, by the way, he's obsessional about privacy so he'll sport my oak.'

The oak, an additional outer door to a set of rooms, usually stood open, latched back against the stairhead wall; when closed – sported – it was a 'Do not disturb' notice.

I turned back to the fire, picked up the shiny steel poker and pushed it between the horizontal bars of the fire basket and raked the coals and watched new flames, yellow streaked with grey and blue, lick through the dull red interstices to the top. I thought about 'rosebuds . . .', and looked round at the magnificence of Bill's state. A walnut bookcase, diamond-glazed, held leather bound books tooled in gold with the family crest. A row of silver beer mugs gleamed on the mantelpiece. Walking sticks with handles of ivory or silver protruded from a cylindrical stand of ebony struts bound with broad silver hoops. A gun case peeped out from behind the mahogany desk. On a sideboard a silver-mounted tantalus, with crystal decanters of whisky, sherry and brandy, stood next to a cigar box inlaid with silver. Here was no shortage of rosebuds.

Insistent at the back of my mind, there had been a question about this encounter. Despite the charm and the shared interest, and the avoidance of politics, had there been an ulterior motive after all? Diffidently, I still thought of these leading figures as being purposeful in all they did, every word and action aimed at a target. Had I missed an inner meaning somewhere? Could this be a new, indirect approach? Rosebuds. Take what is on offer while you can. Pleasures of the flesh and the fleshpots. But where was the connection with the Party?

The speculation was not fanciful. The Party's conspiratorial ethos, familiar to *me* – and suspect – ever since Bernard's return from Spain, was meat and drink to the initiates in the university; for some of them, I felt, it was a prime attraction, joining them to a secret army of salvation. Certainly, Party mandarins were fond of speaking and acting in a style that echoed John Buchan and E. Philips Oppenheim. However, as we can now judge from parallels in Cambridge, it was not always play-acting.

I refilled my cup and cut a slice of the fruit cake, rich, glutinous, perfumed with brandy. There was a sound behind me. The door swung open, and I heard the solid click of the oak being shut. A dapper man in his thirties came in, nodded a greeting, turned and quietly closed the inner door. Lean-faced, tanned, with smooth fair hair, blue eyes, he moved with the relaxed poise of the good games player. He was dressed well but quietly in grey double-breasted suit of good cut, white shirt with fashionable semi-stiff collar, dark blue tie, shiny black shoes. In the university milieu, one might take him for one of the younger dons; in the commercial quarter of a city, a rising young bank official. In either setting you would pass him by without a second glance.

He introduced himself as Peter Pastern, the manner recalling Bernard's clipped soldierly style after Spain. Seated in the chair opposite he helped himself to tea and toast. The tray, I now noticed, had been set for three.

'Heard about you,' he said. 'Come to think of it, I ran across a Glasgow chap in Spain you might know, name of Bernard Lipchinsky.'

'What were you doing there?' It seemed obvious that he had not been on the Republican side.

He did not answer but concentrated on cutting a large piece of cake and, with a hand under it to catch falling crumbs, transferring it to his plate.

Settled into the deep chair, in the easy manner of someone bringing an old friend up to date with his doings, he talked of wanderings in India, Africa, the Middle East, apparently the patrician traveller; but there were hints of imperial *realpolitik*, of the interest of people in high places. Some quality, a magnetism, something supremely self-contained about him, recalled Jimmy Robinson at the socialist camp at Carbeth, charismatic veteran of the Wobblies, with his faith in salvation for the workers through bomb and gun. There was the same kindliness paradoxically joined to ruthlessness in pursuit of a cause, above all the same wonderful certainty that had drawn us young disciples across Carbeth Muir on those summer nights long ago – not so long ago! – to Jimmy's general store in the old bus body under the oak tree, to sit at his feet. Only the cause these two men fought for was different.

Deferentially, the green Candide, I waited for the chance to ask how he had come to meet Bernard, how he knew of my friendship with him, and of my Gorbals history. Skilfully, firmly, he seemed to anticipate the questions and blocked them in advance.

He refilled his cup, and sat back and looked at me appraisingly, blatantly so, wanting me to know it.

What he now proceeded to unfold, in careful stages, was so unexpected, so momentous, at once shocking and exhilarating, that I was torn away from all earlier thinking, and I knew I could never return – as when I had opened the scholarship letter from Oxford. Engraved on my memory I can hear his voice still.

The full intention did not strike home at once. He began with hints.

I keep a look-out, he said, for chaps with special talents for special work. Your Gorbals background makes *you* special. Here in Oxford you're crossing the class divide and you'll *never* make your way back. But you have brought with you a fund of rare knowledge, I should say understanding, about the other side that could make you worth your weight in gold – in the *right job*. And the rewards are high. I happen to know people who could use you. But I must be sure. So we shall need to talk a lot more.

I tried to appear blasé, to hide shock. Among the possible meanings, one was clear, a vision magically made real – the first sign that my coming to Oxford might earn me a better living than I had left behind in the Gorbals; my achievement at last measurable! Here, thrown at my feet by a quirk of fortune, could be the answer to what was poisoning the hours with Rachel.

Were it not for her insistent entreaty to set up house with her, it would have been easy to continue to postpone all thought of what I would do for a living after Oxford. Absorbed in this new life, tasting freedom, all curiosity enjoying free rein at last, there was time enough, surely, two years at least? Sometimes I caught myself trying to copy the carefree attitudes of the others round me, and reminded myself that I lacked the cushioning *they* possessed – secure signposts, links to some vocation, the services, the law, the City, the landed interest. To the question: 'What are you going to do when you go down?' they could unhesitatingly say 'I am *going* to do . . .' instead of the uncertain 'I *hope* to do . . .' It was hard not to envy them.

In these last weeks, trying to cast my thoughts so far ahead had been depressing. Where should I begin, what aims should I have, what must I offer to an unknown market? In the Gorbals vocabulary, 'career' had only an ironic meaning, if it had one at all. Notions of a career had no place in the mission that Bernard's dying father had handed to me, to carry the torch of enlightenment. I was haunted by that last scene in the Lipchinsky's kitchen, the old man bravely sustaining hope, battling with disappointment, coughing blood. I was a fortuitous Hamlet wrestling with that blunted purpose, and now fearing it. I now *knew* that I lacked the certainty it demanded – as I had even then dimly suspected. I had been born with too many doubts. The more I read and pondered and talked far into the night, the more the unanswered questions taunted me:

> '   . . . but evermore
> Came out by the same Door wherein I went.'

There was a comic irony in this puzzlement over *what* to do. I did have a choice! In my simplicity that came as a shock; I remembered with shame my enraged response, a new arrival here, to Crossman's question 'Why do people work?' – when I had said 'Because they'd starve if they didn't.' One day I would have to summon the courage to go to him and apologise. Oh yes, I knew so much more now. Nothing would ever be as black and white as I had hoped.

Pastern must surely know a lot about me to be able to say 'you're crossing the class divide.' I was not aware of doing that, except super-ficially. It seemed to me that I possessed only a provisional identity on this side of the divide – the boss class side – given me by this place. As Alec had foretold, I was here on sufferance, tolerable only if I steeled myself not to think about it. Pastern, in making that remark – airily, but with sympathy – had touched on a question that I shrank from thinking about, even in the most searching moments at dead of night: what *had* I come here for?

Leaving aside the fulfilment of fantasy, romantic dreaming, the lure of adventure, I really had no idea. To change into another person? Very well, what was the change to be, from the ragged, directionless Gorbals boy – to what? The questions 'who', 'what' were unanswerable, especially 'who'. Yet if I could not answer them I could answer nothing of import-ance. It would be years, too late perhaps, before I understood that 'who' was in truth the *only* important choice life asked you to make – if choice it was.

Yet surely the day must come when I did know *who* I wanted to be, and therefore *where* I wanted to go? Till then, whatever Pastern offered, why look at it too closely? Take it with both hands and be glad of it!

With remarkable appropriateness, that very morning had brought yet another revelation. A letter from Bernard had come. Bernard wrote few letters. The man of action preferred to send laconic signals. If he unburdened himself, it was in speech, forced out of him, settling accounts with himself – and then, like a soldier who has halted on the march, he shouldered his burdens once again and trudged on. Here, then, at a distance, being forced to write at length, the occasion must be momentous. Yes. His father was dying.

I was drawn back to that last meal in his house, while I was still not sure whether I dared take up the Oxford scholarship. Even then the saintly old man was sinking, coughing blood. Master cutter, aristocrat of the tailoring craft and paragon of the working-class intellectual, he had striven all his frail life for his faith – gentle anarchism. He was writing a great work on the subject, knowing then that he would never finish it. At the thought of my going to Oxford I remembered how his eyes had blazed in vicarious glory, for in me he saw *himself*, and what he might have been; and surely now, he silently said – appealing to me – I would take up the torch of human betterment that he must lay down?

'He keeps talking about you,' Bernard wrote. '"What is he doing; where has he got to?" For God's sake, what does he expect of you? Of any of us? How can I tell him what's happening to the world? It hurts to see him dying in delusion, but if there was nothing I could tell him when he was strong, what can I say to him now? Well, he's had his run. He's done his best – I suppose. That's all there is to be said. My heart tells me that it's just as well he doesn't see what's coming; after all he's done, after all his hopes.

'Now listen to me. I don't want you to come back here for the funeral, d'you hear? You *must not* waste the time and money. Things are moving so fast, your time there may be short. Anyway funerals don't benefit the dead and I've seen plenty of death, as you know. All that talk of respect for the dead! I wonder what any of it means. What you didn't give them in life it's too late to think about. What the living get out of a funeral God alone knows – maybe settling scores with themselves? Maybe thanking their stars that *they* are still alive?

'I've got to come down to London soon. I'll come and see you.'

My first reaction was relief – and I would remember it forever with shame. I would never have to admit to the old man that I had failed him. Perhaps he already guessed, hence his anxious questions about me? Never again would I have to look upon that sadly slender figure, in the finely tailored clothes that those long spatulate fingers had sewn, the lofty brow crowned with bushy white hair, dreamy eyes probing straight through me to his distant visions. He was too gentle a soul ever to have reproached me, but I would have felt the hurt within him. I knew that I would think of him often in the years ahead, and guilt would return.

Bernard's harsh tone, hand in hand with his grief, shocked me at first. And then I understood. The desperation of the time scourged us both. Perhaps we *were* more sensitively attuned than others? We were not aware of that. In youthful imagination we saw ourselves, and our feelings, as symbolic of the age. We did feel the weight of the world on our shoulders. We knew each moment to be of epochal significance. We viewed everything *sub specie aeternitatis*. And Bernard, therefore, from within the ruins of *his* beliefs, could contemplate his father's life steadily only by traducing the faith that had blighted it, and which retained its meretricious hold even in these his last days. And they might be the last days for all of us.

And then I did weep for the old man, for Bernard, for us all.

Had I been pretending all this time? No. I *had* tried to believe in the old man's gentle creed of perfectibility. Yet here I sat in this opulent room, the fruit of capitalist ruthlessness, and listened to Pastern's gospel with something like welcome in my heart, the relief of a tired wanderer seeing a sure landmark at last – devil·take the hindmost, the voice of that Victorian bridge across the Clyde! I was telling myself that I no longer cared. How could I do that?

Bernard's desolate words burnt into me. Maybe there *was* nothing else? Maybe it mattered little if you tried to change *nothing*? If so, did choice matter? Yes it did; it must. But where? How? The answer would come. I must wait.

Pastern would not be pinned down. He needed more time. As he was in Oxford only briefly, would I dine with him that evening? We would meet in the lobby of the Clarendon Hotel. As I got up to go, he said: 'I'll stay on for a few minutes – I must write Bill a note to say I'm sorry I missed him.'

Plainly he did not want to be seen leaving with me.

The Clarendon Hotel was a sedate place of mahogany and red carpet and dim yellow lighting, whose waiters in shiny black suits recalled cartoons in old copies of *Punch*. I arrived punctually, but seemingly too early. Pastern appeared at my side. I learned in subsequent meetings that he had a gift of materialising out of thin air. 'D'you mind if we don't dine here? I thought it might amuse you to come to a club where I belong – we call it the Explorers. Limited membership, simple but acceptable food, above all privacy!'

I wondered why he had not asked me to meet him there in the first place – another secretive quirk?

We stopped at a doorway and pulled at an iron knob in the brickwork, and far away in the depths a bell clanged and echoed. Heavy footfalls thumped on stone steps within; a brass grill slid back and was quickly shut. The door was opened by a large square-faced man of about forty in a dark suit, whose aspect suggested the ex-boxer.

We went along a flagstoned corridor sombrely lit by electric candles on brackets high on the walls, hearing low voices from deep within the building, up an austere stone staircase, and entered a small square room with blackened beams, oak panelling, and buttoned leather benches against the walls. A shallow shelf running round the room was lined with pewter beer mugs, each engraved with copperplate initials, some with crests. Several square oak tables were laid, but I had a feeling that we were to have the room to ourselves.

Pastern said: 'We've got hold of some audit ale. Care to join me?'

Idly I wondered how they had come by audit ale, only served, as far as I knew, in college.

The ale was brought to me in a guest's tankard, the first time I had ever drunk from silver. As the rim touched my lips, thin and cold, the inner surface gleamed with an aloof, hermetic light. I thought of the cracked enamel of the mug of tea that had been my welcome at Jimmy Robinson's door under the oak tree at the socialist camp at any hour of the day or night – as uplifting as ambrosia from the golden cup of Zeus himself. I had travelled a whole world away, yet it seemed that I had not moved at all.

Yet I had. That evening brought further shocks, though at the time they were muted – possibly by the potent audit ale, pungent, faintly aromatic, dark as the river waters had been that afternoon. Or perhaps the atmosphere of unreality, of miracles, that had attended my coming to Oxford, had lingered in my mind ever since, and taught me to be sparing of astonishment? I cannot remember being shaken – though

I was when I thought about it later – when Pastern casually proposed that I should join the Communist Party and work within it, in secret, for the forces of law and order, in effect to become one of the Party's own favourite weapons, the 'underground member', in the fight against it! Ordinary decent men and women deserved to be protected against the poison in the body politic, and it was the duty – in fact a noble and historic vocation – of the honest man, men like us, privileged and with a sense of right and wrong, to do whatever was necessary to accomplish it. Some of the methods might appear dishonest, but used in a disciplined fashion for worthy aims, they were surely justified.

In the blink of an eye, unaware of the instant of transition, I had stepped through a magic mirror to find myself behind and beyond the façades of the known world where, between the shadows, was the ambiguous one of *Greenmantle* and *Ashenden*. I had been rubbing shoulders with it unawares. It seemed that it had been stalking me! And now, for its own mysterious reasons, it made itself known.

As he talked, I thought of Bernard in Spain, threading warily through that world of intrigue and double-meaning and danger, a vision I had accepted at the time but only in the abstract, something to be wondered at. It was a wonder no longer. It was the real world after all.

If I played my part well, Pastern said, the organisation he spoke for – not named, but linked in some way with government – would admit me into an élite body of men dedicated to defend the Englishman's liberties. When I went down, I would be found a job consistent with the 'underground' role; there would be travel, perhaps some glamour, good pay. Unfortunately my work would *always* be secret.

'Look,' he said, 'it's nearly end of Term and nothing much can be done during the vac. May I be frank? Money's tight with you I know. When you start with us next term, my budget allows me to advance you a hundred – in cash.'

He leaned back and watched it sink in.

I could live well on that hundred for a whole term and more. How easy things *could* be. My head was spinning with visions.

He leaned over. 'By the way, obviously you don't talk about any of this?' Unexpectedly he grinned: 'No one will believe you – and I can guarantee that you won't be madly popular with the authorities.' He shrugged. Enough of that side of it. Don't forget that hundred in cash.

Talk of betrayal made me think of Bernard's letter. I had betrayed his father's trust – whether through sloth or lack of faith made no matter – and that was bad enough. To join the Party and betray it for *money* was unbelievably worse. Apart from that sense of guilt, what retribution might come if I was unmasked! I felt the sweat of fear, sensing merciless forces closing in. Now, at last, I understood the fear that had stalked Bernard in Spain. This world of Pastern's gave off the rank smell of death.

I tried to steady my voice. 'When do you want to know?'

'I'll get in touch.' A hardness had crept into his voice. He rose: 'By the way, would you mind terribly if I asked you to find your way out? I have to make one or two telephone calls.'

I descended the monastic staircase, with a sense of invisible harness binding me to the room behind me. I heard the distant voices in the building but met no one, and was thankful.

I was desperate to talk to someone. Bernard was the only one I dared trust.

9

Beveridge: the Happiness Calculus

Sir William Beveridge held weekly court for selected students from various colleges. Though his hair, brushed flat and slanting across the forehead, was nearly white, with his fresh features, thin face and beaky nose, he contrived an air of youthfulness. With the same intention perhaps, and to offset the effect of a dark business suit, he often wore an informal striped shirt with attached collar, and an even more unconventional red tie. The tie, one suspected, was a signal of solidarity with the forces of progress, a milder version of Crossman's sartorial slumming. Outwardly breezy, he was in essence the iron technocrat. He conducted the group's discussions in the manner of the commanding administrator he essentially was; he dealt with topics briskly like items on a packed agenda, speared each topic or problem with Mephistophelian glee, disposed of digressions or weak objections with a sharpshooter's panache – not that these were frequent, for the intellectual level was generally high – and with a final razor-sharp verdict tossed the item into an invisible 'Out' tray, and moved smartly on to the next.

As a reformer he was much more dynamic than G. D. H. Cole, but unlike Cole it was the administrative challenge of a social problem that was its prime attraction, justice less so; he had little patience with speculation about the long-term human effects of the solutions he favoured. Judging by his stock responses when such questions were raised, one suspected that he either did not understand them – unlikely for such a giant – or was no longer flexible enough to examine the received progressive wisdom. At bottom he was perhaps not truly a reforming spirit at all, but attracted far more by the virtuoso charm of achieving administrative excellence. He saw social problems with the eye of an engineer – as friction in the system. He lacked Cole's willingness to tailor policy to fit the imprecise philosophy of man. That was Cole's golden, endearing quality; but alas it made it impossible for him to present simple solutions to anything, seeing too clearly that social mechanics alone could not address the complexities of human aspirations. That, of course, was far from being Cole's 'defect' alone – it was a perplexity as old as man! The Thirties, however, was a tired epoch – people hungered for simple answers. So Cole had to decline as a prophet, as Laski would for similar reasons; and Beveridge's star would rise.

Beveridge must have had a premonition of his coming role as the high priest of welfare, for the subject figured large in our discussions. Green as I was, convinced still that a fine mind could always see clearly, it was hard to accept that he really did believe, with the early Fabians – as with Bentham – that happiness was *quantitative*, and could be created by bureaucratic fiat. Welfare was palpable and measurable; you produced it, and distributed it, as you produced and distributed shirts or shoes or bread.

One day, impatience overcoming awe, I asked him: 'If the system could so easily be organised to redistribute income, why do we have low incomes at all?'

Unusually for him, he paused to consider. I did not immediately realise that the pause was in part a rebuke; I had interrupted the élite game of social mechanics. He said: 'There are too many people with *low* marginal utility [the comparative value of their "product"], and too few with a *high* one!'

'You mean the "highs" will always have to hand over some of their earnings to the "lows" – a sort of charity? Why not organise society so that the "lows" produce more in value and so get paid more?'

'It is more complicated than that – levels of thrift and prudence, for example, enter into it. But, yes! You may be right – in the very long run. But that's like waiting for the Messiah! We must organise an efficient welfare system before it's too late.'

The boss class was fearful. The dam might break.

I was stung by his reference to prudence and thrift. Even now, as I write in 1987, suggestions that hardship among the lower orders results from their improvidence are made with caution, if at all. Beveridge was speaking in academic shorthand, but the traditional sentiments of the boss class were there too, plainly shared by the others in the room. His words recalled the classic sneer in Glasgow at mention of better housing for the lower orders: 'If you gave them bathrooms they'd use the bath for keeping coal in!'

I persisted: 'Can't we *ever* level up?'

'I have my doubts.'

Surely, I wondered, even with massive transfers from 'highs' to 'lows', complete 'welfare as of right' could never pay for itself? The poor would always be less well provided for than the rich? The Poor Law principle of 'less eligibility' would remain. Beveridge seemed to think this would not be so. Not daring to put the question directly, I murmured under my breath: 'From each according to his ability, to each according to his need.'

J. P. R. Maud, later Lord Redcliffe Maud, then Dean of University College, sitting near me on the cushioned window seat, inclined his willowy form towards me and said smoothly, addressing me but facing Beveridge, 'I don't think Sir William is thinking of implementing Marxism by stealth, are you, Master?'

Maud was warning me to shut up, but I was too green to see it. He was right. Who was I to imagine that I could drive the great Sir William Beveridge into a corner?

'Of course not,' Beveridge retorted. 'That formula's impossible anyway. State welfare must pay its way.'

Tea was served in fluted Leeds china. Beyond Maud's head in the window seat, through the little square leaded panes, I saw the quad thronged with men returning from games, tired, slouching in mannered languor, their murmurings sleepy in the torpid air. Diffused sunlight bestowed on sleeping Cotswold stone a down of golden velvet. I wanted to correct this vision, cancel that insouciance which I could not share, inject reality, *my* reality. I tried to recall the factory, and feel the steam and the noise and the sweat – yes, and a fatigue quite different from that of the slouching games players in the quad. But I could not.

I looked round the panelled room, at the eager, lank-haired, well-nourished men in shining brown brogues and well-tailored tweeds and flannels, deferentially hanging on the great man's words. Beveridge caught my eye, and with a slight movement of the head beckoned me, at the same time disengaging himself from the courtiers. Pink face lit up by his thin, Cheshire Cat smile, but the hawk-like eyes watchful as ever, he took me aside, leaning towards me to exclude the others. 'I know how keen you are and it's a refreshing quality. But let me put the point beyond doubt. No one will get something for nothing – except in the "swings and roundabouts" sense. The aim is not, to destroy inequality. That can't be done. Inequality will always be with us. It is, to put it bluntly, simply a more efficient method of *compelling* people to make wise provision for their own emergencies and for their future!'

Bernard was arriving that day on his promised visit. I felt as though the Gorbals, my old life, was coming to visit me, a meeting with my submerged self; and the prospect may have produced a recurrence of exile's fatigue, the strain of contending with the alien culture.

I wondered, with resentment, whether these smooth people round me, cossetted all their days, ever felt insecure? It was silly to be wounded by their settled attitudes and manners, their inability, or unwillingness, to meet me half-way. They might say, of course, 'Why should we? *You* came here to be with *us* – not the reverse!'

With Bernard I could share thoughts freely.

What would he think of Beveridge's dismissal of 'levelling up'? Bernard, I reminded myself, now the dedicated union official, must be fully committed to that gradualist route. Certainly the Party, typically vengeful towards an erstwhile leading member who had lost his faith, vilified him on that acount as a reformist traitor to the working class.

No doubt he saw the irony of that – many ironies. In his Party days he had not scrupled to attack others in the same fashion. Beveridge's words, he would see, underlined a strange coming together. The Party and the boss class were united in opposing levelling up, the one for Machiavellian motives – the workers must not be allowed to believe they could get 'betterment' without bloodshed on the barricades – the other because of a different, ruthlessly realistic view of life itself; Beveridge would say the *only* honest one.

Beveridge breathed the optimistic but severely righteous middle-class air of the high Victorian epoch that had bred him. Born in Bengal into the proconsular tradition – his father had been a judge in the Indian Civil Service – he expressed inherited attitudes. You prescribed for the lower orders, as was your right and duty, but *your* team must remain on top! Life was necessarily hierarchical. Any other view was hopelessly impractical.

For old Mr Lipchinsky – Bernard's father – levelling up had been a visionary ideal, essential to his gentle Kropotkinian faith. For Bernard it lacked the revolutionary glamour of the faith he had lost; but until he could think of something better, it would have to suffice.

A different disturbance raged within me every hour of the day – thoughts of Pastern and his offer. A demon voice would not be silenced: 'Decide! Decide! Where's your courage?' Courage for what, to sell my soul? So Faust must have scourged himself to the brink. Zest for work and play vanished. Writing an essay took a whole day instead of a couple of hours. I read and re-read a page of a book for hours without absorbing a single word, sat up late and accomplished nothing, walked alone, endlessly, in the murmuring summer air by the green river; saw less of Rachel.

Pastern's proposal, that I should join the Party and work within it as a secret enemy, demanded a passion I did not possess; but what repelled me most about it was that I would have to feign beliefs, deceive people to win trust. When I thought about it, however, I had to ask myself: was I not doing exactly that here in Oxford, seeking acceptance by counterfeiting manners, attitudes, even values, that were not mine – walking among these people and yet not of their world? And never would be? Ah no! In such deception, if that was the right word, there was no hostile intent, as there was in Pastern's plan; the sole aim was to make *myself* understood, and in turn understand *them*.

These scruples, and others too, seem juvenile in retrospect, but they carried seeds of maturity. Pastern's offer of money, dizzying riches to me, stank of the corrupt values that repelled me in this place – boss class people poisoned by worldly ease, their arrogance founded on money. Yet that was the road I too would follow, if I agreed to work with him.

As for his threat, I tried to imagine how Meyer must have felt when the menodge men 'invited' him to join them, or else. What could Pastern do to me? Could he, as he had hinted, contrive a scandal that would get me sent down? Mrs Grundy's influence was still powerful, secretive and, of course, hypocritically selective. One felt it in the air. Reports ran through the junior common rooms with the speed of drums in the bush: Mr X had resigned his fellowship because packets of french letters were found in his rooms; Tony Y., brilliant student, had been sent down when his girl friend's parents complained to his college that he was 'consorting with her immorally'. A few left-wingers, in transient rebellion against their class, murmured that his college might have taken a different view had his family been richer, or more elevated, preferably both. A case in point was Pippa, an aristocrat, who sat her Schools six-and-a-half months pregnant; her condition had been obvious, of course, for some time, but the story was put about that she concealed it so successfully that her college tutor remarked in hall, in seeming innocence, 'What strange clothes Pippa wears these days!' The vandal excesses of the Bollinger would never have been tolerated if class and money had not given them protectors in high places.

I could look to no such natural allies here. Pastern could be relied on to invent a story the authorities would accept without question. He and his cohorts belonged to this system. They knew the ropes. I did not. I would be in a minority of one.

The summer term was well under way and still there was no sign, no word. Yet I sensed his presence. Any day, any moment, I expected to turn a corner and meet him face to face, catch sight of him browsing in Blackwell's or strolling in Christ Church Meadow. Once, going into Fuller's tea shop in Cornmarket with Rachel, I glanced back and thought I saw the dapper form slide past the window outside. At the sailing club, Bill Challoner greeted me affably and talked of many things – never politics! – but Pastern's name was not mentioned. Perhaps the whole affair had been a practical joke, and I would never hear of him again?

'You will,' Bernard said. 'He *always* means business. I wish I knew why he mentioned *me*.' He glanced round warily.

We were in a punt on the Cherwell, and had stopped in the Parks near the slender high-arched foot bridge. It was early evening, the river almost deserted. Slow water gleamed under slanting sunbeams in a vista of gently sloping green banks, tree-lined in the distance. Frail curtains of sun-filled weeping willow hung low – scent of cherry and syringa. Distant voices and laughter and whispers floated down the stream. Sprites danced in the air. This world, surely contained no danger?

In the only other craft in sight, a punt some thirty yards away, a man in white flannels and long-sleeved white shirt lay on his back, his head propped up on the cushioned back-rest. His boater, with a dark blue ribbon, was tipped over his nose; an open book lay face down on his chest. He seemed to be asleep. The punt had been unoccupied when we moored. He must have been strolling on the bank and returned unnoticed.

To my short sight, with so little of his face in view, he was no one I recognised.

Bernard studied the figure, then leaned over to me and whispered: 'Can you get this thing away from here quietly?'

I unhitched the leather strap from round the dug-in pole, swivelled the pole free and pushed away at right angles for a quick turn into the middle of the channel where the bottom was hard and one could pole strongly. He leaned back on his elbows on the buttoned cushion of brown moquette and watched me. The blue jowls wrinkled: 'You've gone native, and no mistake!'

We drew in under the bank near the tennis courts where, it seemed years ago, I had first met Werner. Despite the lengthening shadows, the soft light now diffused, some courts were in use; the noise of play would be cover enough.

'Last time I saw him,' Bernard said, 'he had a moustache, but it's him all right. Still, it's worse *not* to know you're being tailed! What I don't understand' – he pushed out his lower lip – 'is that he's taken no trouble to conceal it. He *wants* us to know!'

Bernard's manner told me that he too needed to unburden. Something had resurrected the deep bitterness he had brought back from Spain. I thought of that first talk soon after his return, on a cold morning in Castle Street with the pavements deep in half-melted snow, when by ironic chance we had sheltered from the sleet in a close a few yards from the Party offices. In the grey desperation of that Glasgow scene, the inferno of Spain possessed us both. Its tortured logic fitted. And now, even in this Elysian setting, unimaginable to me then, every word cut deep – deeper still, coming from a savage world beyond all understanding, all reason. You could not keep any of it at a distance, or turn away from it – the gratuitous cruelty of life, the seeming futility of care, defeat of the heart.

In Spain too, Pastern had trod the shadows; and in his own chosen time he had intervened. I began to see why he had mentioned Bernard to me. He wanted to emphasise his power – over us both.

The Republican intelligence network had taken note of Pastern's existence among the miscellany of foreign camp-followers, journalists, voyeurs, political busybodies, but could not decide whether he was simply another crank fishing in troubled waters on his own account or, as

Bernard concluded, a British agent. How had their paths crossed? Pastern had helped his escape!

Bernard still puzzled over that.

How Pastern knew he was on the run, Bernard never discovered, or so he said. Pastern's money accomplished many things. It found Bernard a hiding place, a little stone house – a herdsman's mountain shelter for the high pasture seasons – tucked away in wild country on the frontier. And it had found the girl to lead him there along ancient unmapped tracks, and hide him and feed him; and after many days in the cramped hut with him, waiting for another moonless night, to guide him across the heights into France. Pastern had been the unwitting catalyst. In those remote waiting days Bernard and the girl fell in love and were happy – despite the unceasing vigilance, the sense of implacable menace.

Night after night, awakening beside her in the pure crystal silence of the mountain, he weighed the temptation to stay – or to take her with him. They were held in a terrible balance. Pastern's money would protect him finitely. If he lingered beyond the allotted time he was doomed; that was certain. If she were caught with him she would die too. Go with him she *must* not; for that would reveal her part in his escape, and bring death to her whole family.

'Et in Arcadia ego' spoke the skull.

Why had Pastern, the dispassionate British agent, gone out of his way to save him, and at so much risk? In the confusion and fear and cruelty of the time, chance discovery, or more likely betrayal, were to be reckoned with at every step, their lives forfeit on the turn of a card, a jealous word, settlement of private scores. The only logical explanation was that Pastern, in the labyrinthine interests of the British secret service, was a fisher of disillusioned men.

Bernard muttered, 'I suppose Pastern's masters ordered him to fish *me* out – instead of other International Brigaders on the run – because a political officer was potentially more useful to them.'

If you agreed to serve them, I thought savagely, as Pastern wanted *me* to do? I could not bring myself to put the question.

Bernard must have sensed it. Abstractedly, he said, 'He got no promises out of me. Let's say I allowed him to hope! I'm not ashamed of that. I was fighting for my life.'

He dug a forefinger inside his shirt collar and scratched the bullet wound, moving the scar-tightened shoulder up and down, while he turned and once again scanned the green river and the leaning foliage. With his back turned to me, he spoke again, and the change in his voice shocked me even before I understood the words. 'A few weeks ago I got an unsigned note – I knew it was from him, don't ask me how; I just knew. All it said was: "There's been an accident. They got to her. I'm sorry." There was no need to tell me who "they" were. Even with the war lost, the Party looks far ahead. Retribution must be exacted *pour encourager les autres!* Pastern himself might have put them on to her, to silence her and destroy that piece of evidence. And maybe to pay *me* out for not being a good boy. I can't be sure. Pastern's lot know how to wait. I *know* how they work. The secret service is a world on its own – it goes on for ever. Some day, they think to themselves, I might be useful to them. That's the way they work.'

We sat in silence. Here on the long slow curve of the sleepy river in its garlands of jewelled foliage, there seemed no place for this dark side of life, only for gentleness, generosity of spirit, hope. I thought of the evening long ago, on the way to his house, when he had first hinted of the existence of that waiting heart on the frontier, his hopes of being with her one day, and with it the overhanging sense of doom awaiting its moment. Yet only an hour or so later, at the kitchen table, his mother innocently pleading with him once again to let her find a nice girl for him to marry, amazingly he had agreed. He had done it, he confided afterwards, to please her. At the time, I had said nothing. He was deceiving himself. Deep down, I now saw, he had been preparing for the worst, hedging his bets. That was a frightening thought. Was hope always so feeble?

Softly he said, his face still turned away, 'I've been lying awake at night chewing over my chances of getting back over there, and carrying a pistol again. Trouble is, without money for palm-greasing I'd be picked up right away. But if I did get through, by God I know who I'd go after! And when I'd paid them back, I wouldn't give a fuck what happened to me. That's all I want now – to get even!'

Without thinking, I said, 'Maybe *that's* why Pastern's reminding you – partly through me as well as sending you that note, if it *was* him – that he's still active, that he still wants to use you? He must know you're not with the Party now, but even in your union work I imagine you could still be of use to him? After all, the Party's active there too. So, if you wanted to get even with them – he might think – you could let him use you after all?'

'I've thought of that,' he said bluntly, closing the matter. He lay there, facing up-river the way we had come, and was silent. He spoke again. The world was folding up like a paper screen. Tidal waves of destruction would soon be hurling us about. How strange that we should still insist, in days like these, on planning for the future? 'Where the hell *is* the future – you tell *me*!'

The unsigned message had reached him about six weeks ago. I shivered. That was about the time I had met Pastern in Bill's rooms.

'You should have told me,' I said.

Bernard was silent for some minutes. Then he spoke in a dulled, distant voice: 'I wanted to hug the misery close. I couldn't have talked about it to anyone, not even you. And then father died a day or two after, providentially you might say. I suppose I hadn't enough mourning to spare. As you can see, I can't talk about it properly even now.'

He sighed heavily and turned round, pulling himself together, reverting to the crisp manner. 'In a way I'm glad the *guerre kilometrique* is nearly upon us. I'd say we have three months left, four at the most. We should have stopped the bastards long ago, before they got strong – instead of deluding ourselves with all that sanctimonious *agitprop* bullshit about peace and disarmament. I went for my medical at Maryhill Barracks the other day. I volunteered soon after we buried father – God rest him – but this Franco bullet did for me. They don't want any wounded soldiers! I'm listed as in a reserved occupation in time of war. Think of that! They're suddenly anxious to keep the workers happy!'

He half-smiled at the thought, shaking his head at the irony. 'As for you,' he went on, 'look on the bright side. With your bad eyes they'll grade you C3, and you'll stay on here.'

His manner had become business-like, incongruously reminiscent of Beveridge. I felt parochial, diminished, far removed from events – from worldly assessments, practical responses. Bernard spoke, as always, from the epicentre of the storm. How remote from lofty Oxford talk in study group and tutorial, the presumption of a godlike view – so beguiling, so flattering to the ego, so misleading!

It occurred to me that for years I must have seen in him the older brother, who would have bridged the distance with father, helped me make sense of the world, whom I would have honoured and trusted and copied. I saw that the attributes I wanted to copy had become fewer over the years; there was one now, precious above all – *competence*, the sureness that moved at once from thought to action. That quality was not diminished by his present disillusion, the veering compass needle. Those were surely the occupational risks of *living*. If only some miraculous contagion would give it to me, then I would be *in* the world always, instead of waiting in the wings for certainty to come to me. That was the quality I had in truth come here to find, inspiration not of the mind but of the spirit. Knowledge was easy. Competence – or was it wisdom? – moved always out of reach, like the grapes of Tantalus. If this was the wrong place to seek it, where was the right one?

'Where is the wisdom we have lost in knowledge?'

'In some ways,' Bernard said, 'it doesn't matter *what* you do about Pastern. If you say "no" I doubt if he'll bother to carry out his threat, war being so close. As for doing what *he* wants, it may be unpleasant but not as bad as knocking your guts out in the factory! And you'll get paid a damn sight more for it. Give your conscience a rest, for Chrissake! These bastards in the Party don't deserve it; they'd have no mercy on *you* if it suited their book. You'll find some of it interesting. You'll make a bit of money, give yourself time to make up your mind what you want to do with your life. As for the girl, if you're worried about accepting her money, my guess is you don't really want her!'

He turned to look up-river again. 'I'm going to say some hard things. About this sense of mission of yours. You're over-sentimental; maybe it's the effect of being here. Oh yes, it's nice to think you're carrying a God-given torch of light. I know what that's worth – it's balls! It blinds you to simple things. Father belonged to the age of hope. It died a long time ago. All that's left for us to do is hold on, preserve what's left of the System and stop the mad men taking over. In Spain, when we were in the line, we used to say "Keep your head down while the shit's flying." People like us have got one job to do now and one only – to live through what's coming. If we don't, everything's pointless. It may be pointless anyway, but I don't want to believe it.'

There was a sad irony in the words 'People like us'. He still thought, as his father had done, that we were the elect, the gnostics, who saw more, saw further, than the rest. If that was true, then God help the world.

It was nearly dusk. We were about to move away when Werner's voice hailed me from beyond the shrubbery leading down from the courts. He emerged, spruce as ever in immaculate whites, racket and a box of tennis balls under his arm, followed by Hannah. Her fair hair streamed smoothly down, tightly framing her face, and rested, curled inwards in a scroll, on the shoulder-straps of the box-pleated tennis dress. The bloom on her full lips matched the glow on her cheeks. At her throat hung a gold Shield of David – then rarely seen in jewellery. As I introduced Bernard, they regarded him curiously, a shade disapprovingly. His blue serge business suit – here on the river! – betrayed him as someone who did not belong. Naively I was stung to say something to mark him out as no ordinary person. With vicarious pride, I said he had fought in Spain. Werner stiffened and looked about him uneasily.

'On which side?' he asked.

Bernard snapped: 'On the anti-fascist side, of course.' He tightened his lips and gave a sigh: 'How could a Jew do otherwise?' He pointed to the tattooed number on Werner's forearm. 'I see *you* have good reason not to like the fascists either – or the Nazis?'

He turned to Hannah and indicated the Shield of David. 'Yes, and you too? If the fascists get control here – and it's perfectly possible – *that*' – he pointed at Werner's arm again – 'is what will happen to *us*. And worse.'

I thought Hannah was about to make a frosty reply, then something in her softened. Her gaze fixed on his shoulder, the glow on her cheeks brightening, with a tremor in her voice, she said: 'You were wounded? I *am* sorry. All this shedding of blood. If only we could achieve things without it.'

Bernard, I sensed, was moved not so much by her words as the tone, the concern bridging the distance between them. A flush suffused his ruddy features. He reached out and touched the Shield of David, and said gravely: '*That* dream's going to demand blood – and plenty of it.'

I thought of the many times, as a child standing in the doorway of the Workers' Circle, the immigrants' social club in the Gorbals, when I had heard the sad, yearning talk of the Return, half-hopeful, half-despairing, not truly sustaining the stooped figures huddled round the bulbous coal stove, but a frail bond among historic exiles, and of the heroes – Herzl, Jabotinsky – dedicated to the achievement of the dream: 'Next year in Jerusalem', a distant light forever beckoning. And I remembered the sudden shrug, and a scornful voice saying '*Effsher koomt der Mesheeach!*' [Maybe the Messiah's on his way!]. Even here, in a few élite outposts in North Oxford, the vision passed from dreamer to dreamer. A few years before, the Russians had proposed a Jewish autonomous region in remote Biro-Bidjan, though many cynics condemned the idea as a strategem to attract capital from Jews in the West. But a Jewish state in the ancient holy land itself? That was as distant as the sun.

Werner said, uncomfortably, 'Please, I am not a political person. I am a simple scientist, a guest in this country. I must not express a view.'

Bernard gave a harsh laugh. 'You have already expressed a view by *being* here – simply by having escaped from the concentration camps! And what about the others you left behind? They are silent. They depend on *us* – and that means you too – to express a view! And God knows we'll have to do a damn sight more than that by the look of it.'

Werner's eyes were blank as if in shock. He spoke in a flat voice. 'All I ever wanted was to do my scientific work and enjoy life. What is wrong with that? What can one individual do? Soon my wife and children will be here with me. This is a civilised country. Such things will not happen here.'

Hannah seemed deeply shaken, as if Bernard's unfamiliar, savage sentiments had struck her across the face. She appeared to draw away from Werner and yet to excuse him. Struggling to find words, her eyes filled with tears. Amazingly, for this usually collected girl, she made no attempt to hide them. Her words, when they came at last, emerged clumsily and seemed to astonish her: 'You batter us with light. I am not used to it.'

10

Cassis: Decadent World

Though the war had been so potently expected, the storm cloud steadily darkening the landscape, one part of my mind had refused to believe in its coming until it was upon us. And then, to my surprise, stiffening the spirit to take myself off to the war and, as I was convinced, to death, had been easier than I had thought.

In retrospect it is plain that I chose not to see *anything* clearly as the last peace time days slipped by – or rather I saw with only one part of the mind. We talked of the approaching war, indiscriminately condemned warmongers and appeasers, and tried to believe that the closed-in student life would continue unchanged for ever. Towards the end of the summer term, meeting Bill Challoner at the sailing club, he asked me if I was going to have any free time in the long vac? Free time – our whole life here was free time! Would I care to join him and a few friends at Cassis for a week or two? Nothing grand, just lazing about on the beach, that sort of thing: 'It's rather a select place. Interesting people, friends from the Nest and so forth – none of the bourgeois seaside holiday crowd.'

I had never heard of Cassis, nor of the Nest. The latter, I gathered later, was the kind of night spot where members of the Bollinger might go when out on a 'thrash' in London.

Seeing me hesitate, he added quickly: 'My dear chap, if you're a bit tight at the moment, do let me lend you a few quid. No, I insist! I'm quite sure you'll pay me back later. So that's settled then?'

I was flattered and a little confused. Was the invitation a final mark of acceptance? Had I truly crossed the class divide at last? Or was it yet another piece of patronising? This, surely, would be the acid test. As for being tight for money, I had put aside £12 to see me through the long vacation, if I was careful; but it would certainly not pay for this Cassis jaunt.

Rachel was going with her family to their mountain villa in the Haute

Savoie, and I was to join her there in September. I could go on there from Cassis. It would all fit in neatly.

Cassis was then still essentially a fishing village, but it had been discovered, like Cyril Connolly's Trou sur Mer, and settled by a small number of sophisticated expatriates. It also had a floating population of moneyed drop-outs, identifiable by their garb of fashionable versions of local working-class clothes – espadrilles, rust-coloured trousers suggesting sails and the sea, fishermen's jerseys. Even in late August the place baked under a relentless sun in a sky of blue enamel, the rocks hot to the foot, the air hot to the lungs, the edges of buildings shimmering in the hard brassy light. There was a small harbour for a handful of high-prowed fishing boats, and fronting it a peeling Hôtel du Port and a few bars, open-fronted, their striped blue shades permanently drawn down. A bistro and a few shops – chandlers, ironmongers, domestic supplies, a baker – were scattered in the winding streets behind. In a tiny square was a little church in whose shade men played interminable, enigmatic *boule*. The sea, to my city eyes an unbelievable blue, glowing with a savage hardness, was fringed with tumbled white rocks. Above the village, on an escarpment that gleamed pink in the early morning sun, was a scattering of new-looking villas with walls of dazzling white and roofs of raw red terra-cotta.

By the standards of the foreign denizens, living was cheap. To me it was unimaginable indulgence, lotus-eaters' paradise. Was I truly here? Did the Gorbals exist? Here was a dreamlike progress – initiates moving in an endless minuet of pleasure, capricious tasting of many things, *dolce far niente*, ambience of sunlit grace and easy charm. As if bewitched in an enchanted demesne where the day and the night were as one, they mingled, drifted away together, returned and mingled differently and moved away again to some secret place, a secluded pool perhaps, among the scatter of white rocks to the side of the harbour. Pairings were seemingly ignored the next morning. I was too green to understand, at first, that some of the hectic, unreal, bewitched quality – an improbable, total detachment – in those around me came from hashish and cocaine.

I moved among them with leaden feet. To be fair I was being faithful to Rachel. Apart from that, a hardness about these knowing women repelled me. Avid for 'action' – the coterie word for love-making – their siren call was: 'Fling woo! Come on and fling woo!' Undiscriminating, or so it seemed, they had no time for tenderness, slow-ripening familiarity, sharing visions by moonlight on the edge of the empty sea.

Above the village, overlooking the sea, one of Bill's friends owned the Villa Vallombrosa, with marble swimming pool and wide white terrace, set in a cool grove of pines. In the velvet darkness one night, about a dozen of us sat or reclined on the edge of the pool whose surface, now still as glass, shone with a ghostly reflection of the moon. The cicadas croaked in booming chorus. I was in the middle of the horse-shoe of bodies, in the hypnotic mood left over from a long day in the sun and in the sea. Someone to my right lit up a cigarette that had an unfamiliar, herbal aroma. He took several long draws in quick succession, then to my surprise passed it to his neighbour. She too drew on it several times and passed it on. As it came near, I had a moment of revulsion at the thought of accepting the cigarette, wet with saliva from several mouths. That apart, however, this was obviously no ordinary cigarette.

Drugs were not yet spoken of, or written about, openly. I had no idea what was in that cigarette. Ashamed to show my lack of sophistication I dared not ask. I may have guessed it was hashish. Even if I had known, I doubt if I would have had the courage to appear 'stuffy' and refuse. Despite the unpleasantness of sharing, it would be an interesting new experience.

The cigarette advanced slowly. The next recipient would be the girl on my right, who I had seen in the distance in previous days but never met till this evening – dark, petite, voluptuous, bobbed hair sticking out spikily, in red trousers and a blue zephyr rolled up high to bare her midriff for coolness. She held the cigarette, now much shortened, between thumb and forefinger, inhaled deeply with each draw, then pressed close, her sea-scented hair brushing my face, and put it to my lips, her other hand, fingers spread and vibrant, upon me. The smell of her hot brunette sweat was powerful, ecstatic. The dark world of her flesh sang in my head. I drew on the soggy cigarette; the acrid taste was disagreeable, but there was no other sensation. I took another draw, and the next instant the top of my head was being lifted off, not unpleasantly, and beginning to float away. In a moment all control would go and I would plunge into the unknown. She pushed the cigarette more firmly to my lips. 'Go on!' she hissed with a fine edge of desire. 'It'll *take* you!' Now panic struck. No more! I took the stub and passed it to the fellow on my left, and leaned back to move away from her. Suddenly her taut little form lunged and pushed me over completely, flat on the warm marble, then came down on me, her trousers sliding down over her hips.

The comic elements did not occur to me till much later – my naiveté, my panic. So this was going to be an orgy! Visions raced through the mind, forbidden, magnetic, challenging. Particularly repellent, to judge from the salacious anecdotes that went the rounds, was the virtually inevitable contact, however slight and fleeting, with male participants. If it could be only with women – ah, that would be wonderful!

Around us the somnolent talk had faded, and there was a quiet rustling and murmuring, the small private noises of people changing position close together.

'Not here,' I whispered. 'Let's go . . .'

'Come on! We're nearly there!'

Roughly I rolled away and jumped to my feet and moved quickly to the steps leading down to the driveway and the road. The clamorous creak of the cicadas was suddenly thunderous, reverberating against the walls of the house and the hill behind. Stupidly I wondered why she had said nothing more. I glanced back. Her compact figure, now naked, had entwined itself with the couple who had been on my left. Her trousers floated in the pool.

Heated, angry with myself, I ran down the pale marble steps to the gravelled driveway and stood there for some moments, harsh self-questioning feeding ill-humour to white heat. I followed the winding incline to the road and looked down at the few lights on the quay. Long past midnight, the bars were closed. The village slept. I began to feel shame at my flight from that lovely, eager, siren flesh; my callow nicety. Incongruously I thought of the encounter, long ago, with the prostitutes Kirstie and Jeanie on the steps of Bernard's union offices in the Saltmarket, and my embarrassed reply to Jeanie: 'I don't want it that way.' No wonder Jeanie had been dumbfounded, as the girl up there had been – but momentarily only. Was I making a fuss about nothing? Did I protest too much?

Roused, restless, repentant, I was half-inclined to return to the villa. Would I be ridiculed? Then it occurred to me that, stupefied as they were up there no one would care, or even notice. That settled it. What would be the point?

I leaned on the low roadside retaining wall, the cliff falling away steeply, and contemplated the sleeping world below. The immediate deprivation, the bruised pride, faded, became trivial. A new awareness, still to be understood, asserted itself, as if I had completed a pilgrimage and returned surer, stronger. Never again would I look in wonder and envy at the doings of these people. As if in proof of this conclusion I asked myself – astonished that I did so – how much longer could I stomach their insouciant, aimless existence? I must leave this place.

The night was hot, the air heavy. There was no wind. The sea shimmered silvery under a great moon solidly shining like a newly minted half-crown piece hanging in the sky. The little harbour thrust its arms out black upon the gleaming water like the outspread claws of a crab, one curved inwards within the other. In the stillness the whole world brooded.

And then, startled, I felt a shift in the air, an inexplicable sense of something momentous impending. My eyes were drawn to a patch of rippling silver a few hundred yards off shore that seemed to have become somewhat darker than the rest of the gleaming water. The next instant the silver solidity of the calm water shattered. I thought I saw a long dark shape break the surface, labouring to rise, phosphorescence flickering round it. The hair on my neck stiffened. Seconds later a black shape became distinct, rose higher, and through the clear, silent night there came the noise of turbulent water, and then, in a few moments, the clank of metal. I had never seen a submarine before. Soon, from the blunt protuberance amidships, a dim patch of light appeared; there came the sound of boots clattering on metal, low staccato voices. I remembered that there was a naval base somewhere along this piece of coast.

Why were they surfacing in darkness? And so near land? The questions were irrelevant. The augury was beyond doubt.

I walked down into the village, the road ghostly under the moon. In the narrow streets every window was dark, not a soul about. I went along the narrow outer arm of the harbour to the furthest bollard and there, alone in the night between land and sea, questioned the black shape on the silver water.

Except for an occasional low-voiced exchange breaking the silence, between two dark figures on the conning tower, the submarine could have been a black cardboard silhouette set in the solid silver sea, with no cargo of death within it. How could horror look so peaceful, so gentle, as this shimmering seascape? Only an hour or so ago I had been in fear of – of what? – the trivial decadence at the villa.

I must have stood there a long time. The moon was setting. The silver faded from the sea. As its surface darkened the submarine merged with it till it was nothing more than a deeper shadow, perceived only because I knew of its presence. I turned away and walked through to the pension near the little church, my steps echoing in the silence, let myself in quietly with the great iron key borrowed from the concierge, and tip-toed up the rickety wooden stairs to my room. Before going to bed I packed my rucksack.

Next morning the concierge said I was wanted on the telephone. After the submarine the call was not a surprise. It was Rachel. Her father had decided, war being a matter of hours away now, that the family must all return to London at once; they were closing up the villa. She would leave that day. Was I leaving too? Yes, I would catch the bus to Marseilles after breakfast and get on the first train I could. 'Thank God,' she breathed, 'there's so little time.' We would meet in London; I could stay at their house in Kensington for a while if I liked. I said I would.

Her clear, loving, serious voice ringing in my ears I went down to the quay. The submarine was still there, wallowing in a long slow swell, the grey metal of the casing, and of the gun on the forward platform, gleaming dully in the sun.

A few days before, in a fit of extravagance, I had bought a cheap straw hat against the sun, a poor man's Panama. It was the first article of attire I had ever bought that had only a fleeting practical purpose. Perhaps it affirmed a new vision of myself, my own creation, yet another step towards independence from the past? Alas, the new persona needed far more time than this in which to mature. And now, I told myself, looking at the submarine, time had run out altogether. Suddenly, uncontrollably, I wanted to proclaim something – anger, defiance, disgust at what was happening, contempt for the world, a snarl at the meddling Fates. I went to the outermost ledge of rock, where I used to dive into a deep pool of clear water, a favourite place for sunworshippers, attested by the yellow patches on the white stone where splashes of sunburn oil had stained it. Further out than the projecting mole of the little harbour, it was as near as I could get to the submarine. I stood at the edge and hurled the hat as far out as I could. It floated through the torpid air, turning lazily round and round, and glided to a landing on the water not many yards away. Of course it was nowhere near the submarine, in fact a few hundred yards short. Still, I had made my proclamation.

The few early bathers, drying themselves or lazing on the rock, stared as if I had gone out of my mind. That was how I did feel. In a bitter fashion I was proud of it. A lone swimmer spotted the hat bobbing on the water, rescued it, and swam back to the rock with a skilful one-armed back-stroke, the hat held high: 'Is this your hat?'

'No,' I said, and walked away. Already somewhat ashamed, pride would not let me take the hat back. In any case, when would I ever need a gentleman's straw hat again!

In consigning it to the sea there may also have been a timid attempt at sympathetic magic, propitiating the elements, to let me return one day – fully armed, sure of myself. I knew, and did not know, that the imprint of those days and nights in Cassis would deepen over the years, for Cassis was my first true trial of strength with a sophisticated if decadent world. They illuminated so much that Oxford obscured – a whole universe of nuances, whispers of sensibility, awareness of self. I was too solemn, too fearful of commitment. Some truths were so self-evident that I failed to see them at all – *refused* to see them. I recoiled from awareness because it demanded instant response! Perhaps, in the Gorbals as a child, aware-ness *was* intolerable and I had taught myself to suppress it – and now, learning to be aware was frightening.

After Cassis, if there was still time, I might become freer, let myself go at last, see people in their own timid humanity, lives within lives, layer beneath layer, and warm to them; a slow ascent from the depths of doubt.

Some of those Cassis people would cross my path again and again. Many would not survive the war. One – brilliant, charming, rich, seem-ingly endowed with everything needed to make life fulfilling – would shoot himself. Deprivation was relative, a very personal thing, a state of mind. Perhaps their sensibility *had* been more complex, and more penetrating, than I had thought? In the light of what was in store, they may have been wise to snatch fulfilment, however shallow, from every single moment, each tinctured as it was with sad questioning. And that lovely girl by the pool – who was I to flee from her, least of all to judge her? Yes, Bill had been right after all: 'Gather ye rosebuds while ye may.' I too, convinced that I would not survive, looked upon my return journey to England as a farewell to myself.

I would see those jewelled Cassis days as caught forever in sunlit amber, the players continuing their life of magical make-believe, each hour and minute prolonged to the uttermost, in tenacious simplicity of mind and desire. And I would envy them.

I was never to revisit Cassis. If I had, the golden image would have shattered.

11

Phantom Soldiering: Oxford in War

In the misty autumn air, raindrops suspended in the darkening afternoon, muted echoes of my footsteps were thrown back from walls of low cloud pressing in upon the pollarded willows on either side of the water-fringed path. All other sounds were muted except for the rough drone of heavy aircraft passing overhead, invisible above the leaden cloud, that rhythmically rose and fell and battered the mind with its purpose; bombers drummed their way eastwards to Germany, the imagined sky full of their black shapes of blunted crosses, gravid with death.

Thoughts were muted too, not yet freed from the suspended animation of soldiering. Horizons remained drawn in close, the future conditional.

These lines of close-standing willows leaning over darkened water, their rounded heads blurred in the mist, my first view from the train bringing me back from the army, aptly symbolised the Oxford I remembered, marshy, torpid, drawn in upon itself – and the dim, uncertain world to which I was returning. This had seemed the right place to start, on a deserted perimeter where all was indistinct, to beat the bounds of my new world again; not truly mine but a simulacrum I had fashioned for myself.

Now and then the leaden air was mysteriously moved by a breath from afar, and thick curtains of mist drew aside to reveal spectral trees and hedgerows and clumps of reeds beyond the quiet water on either side of this narrow strip of earth. A few feet away, the dark waters moved with barely a ripple, and softly, with a whisper, lapped the land. Between the trees the path twisted and turned and drifted away among the shadows, seldom visible for more than a few yards ahead. Here and there its surface of beaten earth was worn through, and tree roots unexpectedly protruded and snaked across, iron hard to the unwary foot.

In the intervals between transits of bombers above, the ghostly silence wrapped itself round me like the blanket of clammy mist itself – appropriate too, and welcome, for I needed to understand the fact that I was here at all! The *guerre kilometrique* seemed set for eternity. Few of us had shared the contrived optimism of the short-lived popular song, 'We're going to hang out the washing on the Siegfried Line'. We knew that we would not come back from the war.

Facing life again was an unbelievable anti-climax. The wonder and elation were almost too much to contain – and above all guilt, for there were many people I knew who would not come back; Rachel's memory would return unbearably through the years – and at dead of night I would tread useless circles in my room, stand at the blank window and gaze out at the unfeeling stars, and curse myself for a fool and a coward.

And so I walked here and marvelled once again – but this time for quite different reasons – as I had on my very first arrival in Oxford, asking myself, 'What right have I to be here?'

Bernard's prediction that the army would reject me proved right, except for some delay. I had written to the authorities asking to be called up as soon as possible, and they had done so. There had seemed no point in waiting. Since death was near, I might as well get it over with. In its own good time the army gave me a ticket back to civvy street.

In the still of the night in barracks I had pleaded with the Fates: 'Make Hitler turn eastwards! It's our only chance!' At last, unbelievably, the news came over the radio in the smoke-filled NAAFI canteen in Catterick Camp, barely audible above the din of shouting at the bar and the darts board and the battering of boots on the plank floor, the yelling of orders for beans and chips and 'char'. A shiver ran down the spine – a sense of divine intervention, the momentary fear of an answered prayer.

What an irony – that salvation would come from a titanic clash between two tyrannies that, as oppressors of the Jews, had outdone even the Spanish Inquisition and the Roman proconsuls! No one else heard the announcement, or if they did, took note of it; even though the words, and the portent, boomed out of the sky with Delphian force. I could *hear* the iron thunder of those far-off guns, like the apocalyptic drum beats in the Eroica. I wanted to share the answered prayer. I called out: 'He's done it! It's Napoleon all over again. We can win now!' No one was listening.

Yes, I *had* intended to go down with the sinking world, sad, obscene, despicable. But what now? If I did survive, then maybe there would be enough of the old innocent world left too, to be worth living for?

———

Pastern, after a silence so long that I had ceased to expect any further word, did keep his promise to make another appearance. I told him I would not spy for him. In any case I was going into the army. Unmoved, he became very thoughtful. He would not take my answer as final. As for the army, he had some contacts; it might be most useful if I went into Signals. Whether by coincidence or not, to the Signals I was sent.

Rachel volunteered for a women's auxiliary unit; after a time it became evident, from various small details, that she was on secret work. She never once hinted at its nature, and I resisted the temptation to press her with questions – only much later would I see this reserve, on both our parts, as evidence of trust and love and mutual respect, a solidity that I ought to have valued more, while there was still time. After some months she was posted away, I assumed abroad. She wrote lovingly, but cryptically, from an army forwarding address. And then – silence. War-time Oxford accustomed you to that; people went through a black door, as into a magician's cupboard on the stage, and vanished. She had warned me that the time would come when no letters at all would be permitted, lest a chance clue disclosed too much.

I knew in my bones that this silence was final. Again and again in the years to come I would ask myself whether she would have gone, or so soon, if we had been living together. I think she *would* have gone, in the end; for her it was a personal fight against the forces of evil. On our last weekend at the family's country house, then beginning to fill with staff evacuated from London, she had talked sadly about our life of 'living and partly living'. Oh we could have had a golden time together, happiness greater and deeper than this to remember! In a little while who could tell where we would be?

We peered into the dark future. There might still be a chance. Oh there must be? We must hope for that – and never, ever, give up hope.

She intended the affirmation as a promise; her heart would compel it to come true. It sounded like a farewell.

The time came when she was listed as 'missing'. Specific facts would have given me nothing. I knew she was dead. The family were not unfriendly, simply correct. How much they knew of our poignant tug-of-war there was no hint. Recalling her fierce independence, I imagined they knew nothing. And so we could not even mourn together. What rights had I, having failed her? What mattered more was that I had been untrue to myself, or to what I *knew* of myself. All that remained was to curse my indecision, my self-doubt – or was it simply lack of courage? – for evermore.

Towards the end of the war I would receive a letter in her tiny, rounded hand, one of those wartime 'pre-mission' letters intended for onward transmission only if the writer did not return. Two sentences in particular would burn into my mind, and whenever I thought of them I would hear her voice in my head: 'You suffer because you are the man you are. I did not always know how to give you the understanding you need.'

Far away in the mist voices floated, snatches of disembodied talk, muffled one moment, clear the next, distant whispers, a trill of female laughter, an answering low chuckle, cadence of speech rising and falling, sometimes companionably familiar as if heard through the winding corridors of a rambling old house. They grew stronger, wafted closer by some mystic surge of the floating masses of grey vapour, a timid counterpoint to the undulating drone of the bombers overhead, then were lost again.

Sometimes the voices sounded so near that they seemed to be fragments of an inner colloquy of my own, or echoes of conversations from another, distant time.

Many times, in the army, I had reason to think of Bernard's bitter words on the river – 'deluding ourselves with all that sanctimonious *agitprop* bullshit about peace and disarmament'. Possibly my unit had been issued with older material, so that more favoured front-line formations could receive the best? That might have been why I was carrying a rifle stamped 'drill purpose only' and dated 1900? But why were we still trained in flag signalling, and in the use of primitive buzzer sets, suitable for trench communication, dating from the 1914–18 War? If this was the equipment of the war-mongering country which the Party had condemned for being armed to the teeth and bent on aggression, then God help us!

The nearest I came to battle – though whether it *was* battle I never discovered – was the night of the General Alarm. There was great talk of invasion. The orders were strict. The signal for a General Alarm would be whistles; when we heard them, whatever the hour of day or night, wherever we were – in camp or in the town – we must get to the barrack square 'at the double' in full battle order, with canvas bandoliers of ammunition draped about us, and await further orders. One Saturday night, idly whistling as I prepared for bed, I heard a shout from a nearby hut: 'Hey – shut that fuckin' whistling! I think that's the fuckin' General Alarm!' I stopped and listened. Unbelievably, through the thin night air there came the clear sounds of whistles, frenetically repeated, coming from all directions in the vast Catterick complex. From barrack huts on every hand came a cacophony of shouts and curses: 'Christ this is it! I can't fuckin' well believe it! All right lads, get crackin'! Jerry's on his way!'

Within seconds it seemed, by some miracle – untried soldiers that we were – we were assembled in ragged company formations on the dark barrack square. The coast was not far. It would not be long now before we trundled away in trucks and manned the cliff tops and the beaches with our massive firepower of superannuated rifles! And with any luck we would see Jerry off. There was a curious calm among us. There was no speculation; no bravado.

I cannot remember feeling fear, only impatience for something to happen. And to get it over and done with.

'. . . half in love with easeful death.'

All around us in the black night the whole world had broken into monstrous noise and movement. Trucks and guns rumbled all over the blind countryside. Despatch riders, their thin beam headlights ignoring the black-out orders, darted among the heavier traffic. Planes – ours or theirs? – droned up above. Far to the east, great coronas of light burgeoned and died down. Distant thuds were heard – could that be artillery? Something momentous must surely be going on.

Gaps in the ranks gradually filled as men dragged themselves in from a night out in the pubs and dance halls, and trudged on to the square pulling on their equipment.

We waited throughout the night, standing at ease at first, then slowly subsiding to sit on packs or on the ground. Smoking was forbidden. In the first faint light of dawn, silence returned. Some vehicles trundled back along the narrow roads, but not the great mass we had heard before. Orders came to return to quarters. The General Alarm was over. We went in silence, scraping boots on the ground, too tired for talk – or thought.

———

We were ordered to say nothing of that night. Was it the famous invasion attempt, talked of after the war, from which barges bearing dead Germans were said to have been seen floating in the shallows? The mystery was never lifted.

When it became clear that the military machine was going to extrude me back into 'civvy street', a puzzling depression set in, a sense of wasted time – but more particularly of wasted emotions.

There came a period, seemingly endless, of being posted back and forth across England – like a ball punted about a field simply to keep it in play – and I sank lower and lower into the depths of futility; I might as well be *anywhere*, or nowhere, and the next posting would be as meaningless as the last.

One day the feeling miraculously lifted, as by a healing touch. I arrived in an isolated holding depot in the Peak District, among jagged crags, fast running streams and tumbling, milky falls, reminiscent of the Highlands; perhaps the resemblance worsened my overcast state? I entered the quartermaster's stores, housed in an old dark barn dimly lit by a few dusty electric lamps, its high cross-beams giving the place an eerie, other-world atmosphere, and there in the shadows behind a counter, surrounded by shelving crammed with clothing and equipment, stood Alec.

I would discover that he too was being posted about with apparent aimlessness. Possibly because he was older than most of the current intake, the army seemed reluctant to let him go to a fighting unit; he chafed at being relegated to what some men would have welcomed as a series of cushy billets. Perhaps because of his obvious solidity he had been put in temporary charge of stores. We were all, it seemed, in temporary charge of something – ourselves too. That was war.

For the first few moments, however, we stood there among the dusty mountains of military paraphernalia and gaped at each other without speaking. Once again, no words fitted. He was, if anything, the more shaken, the result, as I was to learn in a moment, of seeing me in such gloom, and seemingly in worse case than he was. He was the first to speak, and the words burst out of him impulsively: 'Christ Almighty, fancy meetin' *yew* here! Yew being a' Oxford, ah thought they'd have put yew in a grand big job by now – orderin' the likes o' *me* abou'?'

I had after all, joined the boss class. How could it be that I too was being shunted about like this! People like him, he seemed to say, had no right to expect anything better. For me, matters should be different. Yet here I was – as he saw it – still an underdog.

The long bony features reddened. Ashamed, he plainly wondered how to make amends. I was more amazed than hurt. The Alec I had known, sensitive, stoical, looking life squarely in the face, was not given to petty spite. Perhaps he was changed too, as I was? The shifting horizons of war, especially the barrack-room culture of grudges and 'ticking' – kicking against the pricks of life – could so easily corrupt. He had let himself down.

He stood, head bent over the counter much as he used to stand over his pressing board across the table from me in the factory. Suddenly he turned on his heel and reached towards a section of shelving crammed with hundreds of pairs of thick grey woollen socks, pulled out a couple of pairs, turned and reached across the counter and thrust them into my hands. 'Here – ye'll need these some time.' Seeing my surprise he rushed on: 'Och, th'army'll no' miss them! Go on. Put them out o' sight.'

Supply and equipment rules being strict, he knew he faced a charge if discovered. His action was not strictly necessary and he probably knew it; I was not short of a pair of socks. But socks had come to his mind first, naturally enough; in our Gorbals life, next to boots and trousers, they were the most important items of clothing. And so the 'gift' of socks, and the risk he ran – though small – took us back to a shared life, joined us as no words could have done. His action conveyed something else. This sympathy, sad and warm and delicate, could not say everything – far from it. We both knew it. At the very heart of life the world had turned its back on sympathy. That was the tragedy of all of us. The primeval melting-pot was engulfing us all.

'Aye,' he murmured, 'this fuckin' war . . .' Once again there were no words to fit.

Uttered with such rasping feeling, the curse joined us together even more, affirmed our shared sadness for the world, our defiance of the powers of evil that made it so – and lightened our hearts.

A few days later we both left the depot and went our separate, inscrutable ways. I would never see him again. The next I learned of him was some time after D-Day, when I read the posthumous citation.

The mist drew closer still, curtains of sodden grey cotton wool trailing wisps of vapour, the steamy breath of a giant. It was easy to feel a sense of other worldliness – imagined flicker of marsh gas, suspirations from the dark heart of the earth, myth and magic, sprites and Jack o' Lanterns, spectres of the past and the future flitting between two worlds here brought together.

Army life had drawn down the blinds of the mind; you were in the bowels of the machine. By a caprice of the Fates I *had* come back. And now I must learn to think in the future tense once again. How much of the chemistry of this place would I find as I had left it? How much of the previous 'me' had I brought back? What had been lost? What was new?

The sky was silent. The bombers had all flown on. I heard the voices, closer now. They faded as the mist closed down again. After a while, another movement of air lifted it again, and they were so near that I peered among the shadows, but there was no one. And then, from out of the trees ahead, a twist in the path brought three figures, two men and a girl. One was Bill Challoner, but so changed that in a busy street I might have walked past him unaware – the face drawn and thin, the dark blue eyes sunk deep into the sockets, as if he had retreated into timid old age and peered out from the empty shell of youth. A quiff of hair was pure white, contrasting disquietingly with the remaining fair hair, now dulled, thinner than I remembered it. His left leg was held stiffly as he walked, and he leaned on a thick stick. He wore a long khaki greatcoat over a blue double-breasted blazer and grey flannels, scarlet silk shirt and dark blue silk muffler.

If Bill looked as though he had the mark of death on his brow, the other man, Ivan – whom I had not met before – was the classic picture of vigorous, self-renewing youth, tall, dark, broad, ruddy-featured. The truth would prove to be the reverse. Bill would live on, permanently scarred – in mind as well as body – by his torment in a 'brewed up' tank. Ivan, I would learn, was doomed; he had Hodgkin's disease.

He must have been about eighteen. He was dressed in a long raccoon coat, down to mid-calf, red corduroy trousers and fur-lined ankle boots, and a silk scarf, striped lengthwise red and blue, wound several times round his neck and hanging down below his waist. A bushy moustache gave him an old-fashioned appearance, recalling steel engravings of late

Victorian and Edwardian men of fashion. He walked with a suggestion of a swagger; perhaps he compensated in this fashion, unawares, for the knowledge that his time was short.

The girl was Diana Gollancz, also met for the first time – daughter of the firebrand left-wing publisher and founder of the Left Book Club. The immediate, arresting impression was of her intense, pre-Raphaelite pallor. Indeed intensity was the keynote, questing, indomitable, innocent – a self-wounding innocence. Rich brown wavy hair tumbled on her shoulders and framed her paleness dramatically. She wore a dark blue cloak over chestnut corduroys and a voluminous red sweater. Something about her looked bohemian, an impression soon confirmed; she was at the Slade. Oxford had lost its severe, aristocratic aloofness, and had become a steamy, wayward, cosmopolitan colony of London, with the influences of Bloomsbury, Hampstead, Soho and Chelsea dominant. C. E. M. Joad was to epitomise the change, dismissively, when he referred to Oxford as 'the Latin Quarter of Cowley'.

Ivan, despite a certain defensive exhibitionism, was a gentle soul, of great sweetness of character. He hid his knowledge of the sentence of death. Bill, who seemed to know him well, with characteristic nicety never once, by the slightest hint, drew attention to his condition, or the bizarre background to his presence in Oxford. It was Diana, when we became close, who told me the story, tears in her eyes as she told it, and in mine as I heard it – after his death. It was awesome, with an absurdity that made it the more terrible – and to me amazing, for unlike my Gorbals experience, it had nothing to do with living at the very edge of survival, but with caprice, prejudice, cossetted obstinacy.

Ivan had set his heart on going up to Oxford; no great ambition, for most people he knew did so as a matter of course. His parents, however, strict fundamentalists, apparently saw Oxford as the very pit of iniquity. To go there would be to seek damnation. They must not allow it. Living the life of a chronic invalid, he pined and pleaded. At last, when he had been given at best a year or two to live, his parents relented. Perhaps, knowing now that he would not be able to taste Oxford to the full, they could let him go with a lighter heart?

He tired quickly. He devoted what hours he could, and his ample funds, to being a dilettante aesthete.

Diana had been drawn to him in mystic sympathy, compassionate tenderness, love that was forfeit from the start. She watched over him, sat with him on the days when he lacked the energy to get up, listened, followed his whims – *cared*.

Bill's voice was a shock. Remembered as deep and resonant – he had sung baritone in his college choral society – it was croaky, unsteady, the voice of a very old man. Seeing my concern, he grinned deprecatingly, as if to say 'I'm still alive, am I not! What more can one ask?' After the introductions he turned to me. 'I did hear that you were coming back. Must say I never expected to fetch up in *this* place again!'

Incongruously, those words must have triggered some remote connection in my mind, awaiting its cue. His part in the Pastern affair clicked into place. It was *he* who had been Pastern's spy in the university branch of the Party – well-camouflaged as a mandarin! When Bill had been about to go down at the end of that last summer term of peace, he must have suggested to Pastern that I was the right person to be infiltrated as a replacement. Many years later, meeting Pastern by chance in the Sind Club in Karachi, I taxed him with this interpretation. I hardly expected him to confirm it, but he did not deny it. As for Bill, though we became good friends as the years went by, he never once, even indirectly, referred to the episode.

Bill said, 'I suppose they've sent me here to convalesce in comfort.' Thoughtfully he added, 'I didn't want to come back here. The course I'm on is just an excuse.'

I would find that Oxford was full of service people on courses; if a course was ill-defined, or dismissed as of no importance as Bill had done, it must be secret! When he was not at the Radcliffe Infirmary for treatment, he divided his time between Bletchley Park, supposedly occupied by evacuated sections of the Foreign Office, and what he described as a briefing department at Woodstock; I learned later that the latter was a branch of Intelligence at Blenheim Palace.

'Remember those times sailing on the river?' He grinned feebly, gritting his teeth against the pain from his leg, banging the stick on the ground. 'Funny! I've still got a boat here. With this gammy leg I'm not as nifty as I was . . .'

He left the question in the air, waiting to see if I would recognise it and respond. In earlier days I might not have done. I said I would be glad to take him out in his boat.

———

'A boat!' Diana breathed. 'Oh I'd love to go sailing!'

Bill said I could use his boat whenever I liked.

Ivan, perhaps feeling the need to assert himself in riposte to our maturer attitudes, to him esoteric, struck a declamatory pose, and with music hall fruitiness, addressed the curtain of mist: 'How now mist! Avast there! I command you to listen to the music of the spheres.'

He bent his knees, pretending to sit, stretched his hands over an invisible keyboard, and struck imaginary chords. Diana smiled affectionately and nodded her head, pretending to follow the transcendental sounds.

Bill half-turned away and looked at me steadily. Alas *we* could not share that world any more. What did it matter? Who could smile now? What had been good enough for Dada, as a comment on this world, made just as much sense now – or as little.

Compared to Ivan and Diana we felt old, and were sad with the knowledge. Had *we* had enough time to be young? For our separate reasons we thought not. The differences between us, now, seemed insignificant.

Although I had not been in battle as he had, life in uniform had left a similar stamp on us both. We had returned to this place seasoned in inexplicable ways. We were rougher, earthier, surprised by fewer things. Strangest of all, it seemed that Bill saw *me* differently now. My Gorbals origin was now a bonus! What an irony! After all this time I had spent trying to suppress it, or excuse it – he now saw it, with envy, as an added seasoning of the soul. Before, if that had been said to me, I would have been angry, thinking I was being patronised; now, even if I was, I cared little. There probably was some truth in his impression of me after all. So we were drawn together, sharing a world that was already in the past. We were not as others. We knew what things were like before; at this distance simpler, clearer cut. We were already a generation with no links to the present; and there was no going back. Others would never see our vanished horizons as we could. We were now closer to each other than we could ever be to them – to people of Ivan's age – to anyone! And we had better *stay* close, for there were fewer of *us* with each day the war lasted.

In one sense at least – for what it was worth – I had crossed the social divide at last, as Pastern had said I would.

What *was* it worth?

———

12

Victor Gollancz: Ideals in Confusion

One of my dreams, when leaving the Gorbals, had been the glory of meeting some of the heroes I had humbly read about, who trod the high places of the world, and draw from them a new charge of pilgrim inspiration, a vision of the selfless road ahead. Of the three foremost, I had met Cole; for Laski I must wait and hope; but now, through Diana, I was making the acquaintance of Victor Gollancz.

It was as a prophet, in particular of worker enlightenment, that I had worshipped Victor Gollancz from afar – passionate trail-blazer, bringer of light, powerful champion of progressive thought. His founding of the Left Book Club had been a stroke of genius, epoch-making. With it he made *contemporary* thought, and discussion of great issues of the time, accessible to the lower levels of the social pyramid as they had never been before. The Everyman Library, previously the lifeline of the workers' education movement, had clung to the safe ground of the classics, and near-classics like T. H. Huxley, essentially a view of the past. Those orange limp covered Left Book Club Editions, with their stark, robust black lettering, were carried proudly at left-wing meetings and demonstrations, Workers' Educational Association classes and summer schools, a common recognition signal among 'progressives', badge of a new Enlightenment.

With these visions of him shining strongly in my mind, seeing him in his home setting was in many ways unsettling. The name of his country house in Berkshire, Brimpton Lodge, suggested riches, ample acres, a style of living violently inconsistent with my image of the egalitarian evangelist. To my eyes this Gollancz life was princely – perhaps not as much so as that of Rachel's family, but rich enough; there was, however, an important difference – Rachel's father did not pretend to be anything other than what he was, a rich businessman.

Two features of Brimpton Lodge, a house of sombre aspect enfolded in oaks and beeches, with hummocky country surrounding it, seemed to cast similar shadow over my earlier vision of the man himself – in retrospect perhaps unfairly. In a gallery lined with books, otherwise a graceful setting for browsing and reflection, slips of white paper peeped out here and there on the shelves, in effect loan slips, giving title, the borrower, and the date removed from the shelf. Gollancz entertained a good deal at Brimpton Lodge, and many of the loan slips referred to books that guests had borrowed and taken with them when they departed. On the face of it the record-keeping was logical; still, this blatant evidence that the great man kept careful account of his benevolence smacked of ungraciousness – at best, he could have taken the trouble to be unobtrusive about it. In the grounds, near a mound partly concealed by trees, Diana led me down a flight of stone steps into a smaller version of the underground bunker at Rachel's country home. She watched my reactions, and I was sure that my feelings echoed hers. Why did this air-raid shelter disturb me so much more? Some prejudice, perhaps from the example of Bernard's father, still clung strongly. For a prophet to be self-centred was surely a contradiction – he did not go to great lengths to protect himself and his interests, least of all did he use riches to give himself an unfair advantage in that respect over the common man. As for that other, much more elaborate shelter, there was some excuse – it had been built by a capitalist who made no claims to a highly developed social conscience as Gollancz so blatantly did; indeed Gollancz publicly brandished his social conscience as his *raison d'être*! Yet here was Gollancz revealed far differently, tough, egocentric, looking after number one.

I told myself to curb this naïveté, and not to be mean-spirited either. The Gorbals viewpoint was still too strong. I must stop looking at the world from the bottom of the pyramid.

Diana, though she had no interest whatever in politics or current affairs, could show an intuitive grasp of what was appropriate in public life, and she was sometimes ashamed – though loyally trying to hide the fact – of his more extravagant posturings. In all seriousness he could flaunt a prophetic grandeur, or perhaps it was simply uncontrolled showmanship, which would have been comic in less traumatic contexts: for instance, in the title of his pamphlet on the Nazi brutality to Jews, apostrophising not only Hitler but all other rulers – *Let My People Go* – words befitting a Moses, not a Gollancz.

She treated him with a mixture of reserve and wariness, as one might an unpredictable Caliban. Certainly, when the mood took him he seemed to enjoy playing the role, though it sat incongruously on that fastidious personality, eupeptic, urbane, the chubby features shining with facile amiability, quickly changeable. Crudely aggressive he certainly could be, with an unabashed appetite for power and influence, and an inclination to be a bully not always kept in check, certainly a dangerous man to cross. There any affinity with Caliban ended. Cultivated, responsive, with great sensibility, he could be delightful company.

He set great store by his friendship with Maisky, the Soviet Ambassador since the early Thirties, and would be downcast when it hit stormy waters, for Maisky would sometimes show displeasure at something Gollancz had said or done by failing to invite him to embassy events. When this happened, Gollancz feared that his exclusion would be permanent, and that his public position and influence would diminish in consequence. Seemingly he had not learned that support for Stalin did not earn anyone that prime privilege of friendship – freedom to criticise or hold divergent views. Perhaps he had dreamed of being the favoured Western counsellor to the Russian Bear, and would school him to behave like an old-fashioned Fabian socialist? I wondered how so perceptive a man could be so innocent. At dinner one night, in an aside to Ruth, his wife, Gollancz mentioned one such rap over the knuckles from Maisky, in tones that showed profound hurt. She may have shared my wonder, for she nodded absently, and made no comment. Diana caught my eye and shrugged.

I asked him, 'Why do you care?'

The little moustache bristled. He pushed his lips out in a pout. 'I will not tolerate people trying to control me. Besides, I do genuinely admire the Russians . . .' There followed a startling paraphrase of Churchillian rhetoric about 'our noble allies' and the 'historic deeds of the valiant Red Army'. 'In any case,' he went on, 'I feel it to be my mission to be a bridge between the old democratic West and the new socialist order being built there in Russia. They are making a big mistake, turning away from me.'

I mentioned Stalin's sham-legal murders of his comrades, and his treaty with Hitler. Surely it was interest, not sentiment or principle, that was the essence of *realpolitik*? Was that not also true for the Party here – Stalin's fifth column? The Webbs and Bernard Shaw, and so many others, had hypnotised themselves into believing that Russia was a humane democracy instead of a despotism only differing in style from that of Czarist Russia. Surely *he* saw that?

The domed brow furrowed, and with the wintry vibrations the table was stilled. Had I gone too far? Then he seemed to shake himself, and a smile reached out across the table to me like a great warm handshake; he turned to his wife and winked: 'Not a bad *pilpul*! Yes! In fact a very good *pilpul*.'

In Yiddish tradition the word *pilpul* had many connotations. In the expression 'pilpul-maker', for example, it could imply respect, say, for a scholar; but the word was more often used in gentle teasing, and sometimes, more harshly, to refer to an arid logic-chopper. It was obviously in the latter sense that Gollancz had used it in reference to me. Old enough to adopt the privilege of age towards me, the bully in him had taken over, and he had delivered what was meant to be a crushing rebuttal. After all I was very young, and poor, and he was an important public figure; he had me, he supposed, at his mercy. I decided to stand my ground: 'Sir, calling what I have said a *pilpul* does not diminish the force of it.'

To his credit, he professed delight at my refusal to be crushed. Part of him, at that time in his life at least, was drawn to someone who gave as good as he got. Grinning, he withdrew. I must not think he was dismissing what I had said. He was impressed and wanted to talk to me more fully later.

I had been stung by his introduction of the word *pilpul* for another reason too – not the word itself but the pointed introduction of an irrelevant Jewish context to the conversation. It exemplified a device I had often encountered among assimilated upper-class Anglo-Jews, English versions of Werner's *Hofjuden*. When with Jews they did not know well, wishing to oil the wheels of discussion or lessen tension, they would temporarily abandon the character of the standard Englishman of their class and throw into the discussion a traditional Jewish image or association or trick of speech, aiming to trigger thoughts of shared history and shared emotion and create enough sympathy for the needs of the moment – a cultural trick to gull you into lowering your guard. Gollancz had dredged up the word *pilpul* to show me that within the shell of the cultured upper-class Englishman he was at heart a Jew like me and therefore at one with me. In the act of crushing me he proclaimed that we were brothers. He knew very well that but for the chance of Diana bringing me to his house, he and I could never have met under the same roof – we were light years apart.

In the Gorbals, by contrast, for better or worse the cultural and religious linkages among Jews were real, natural, always present; there was no need to invent them for the convenience of the moment. What angered me particularly, however, was the condescension in his use of the trick. Perhaps I was being too much of a purist? I was forgetting the lesson of Germany; the concentration camps did not distinguish between rich Jew and poor, religious or not.

Lost in thought, Gollancz repeated the word *pilpul* – 'a *pilpul*, yes, a very good *pilpul*'. He savoured it, pleased with himself. Then, good humour restored, he regaled the table with anecdotes about Maisky and the Embassy over the years. However, my *pilpul* must have continued to exercise him; after dinner he took me aside: 'The extreme Left does worry me. I sometimes feel we are all being manipulated by the Party.'

The remark was amazing in view of his long association with the Party in various contexts, in particular the Popular Front and the Left Book Club. Indeed, at one stage many people assumed that the Club *was* a Party front organisation. How could this cultured, worldly wise man, close to great affairs and the rough and tumble of politics, imagine that the Party would not manipulate him as it did everyone else? For a time he had towered in the political arena like a giant; did he dream that he, not the Party, was the stronger? When he opposed the Party, as he did over the Hitler-Stalin Pact, he had been shocked and deeply hurt when the Party and its fellow travellers – such as D. N. Pritt – attacked him. As for Pritt, the rich barrister, elected to Parliament for Labour but whose 'line' was so close to the Party's that a membership card would have made no difference, Gollancz had numbered him among his friends; so the fellow traveller attitude should have been familiar. As for the Party itself, over the years Gollancz had had many dealings with its principals, including Harry Pollitt the leader and Palme Dutt its steely theoretician. How could he not know that the Party would react as it did?

That he did *not* know, or behaved as if he did not, must have reflected the heady confusion of the time, when everything, events, attitudes, the positions taken up by people in public life, seemed the products of distorting mirrors, of desperation, a kaleidoscopic charade that would be unbelievable to those who came after.

Sometimes he spoke as if he was the arbiter of rectitude in political and social attitudes – what he did or said must be judged by *his* standards alone. He was genuinely astonished, and bitter, at having been pilloried for his donation to *Daily Worker* funds. Surely a cheque to the Party's paper, he seemed to imply, was as bland an action as supporting any other humane, gentle cause – like the lifeboats or Dr Barnardo's Homes? I asked what he would do if the red revolution came; would he expect to continue in his privileged position?

Thinking back, I must have sounded – on this occasion and on many others – insufferably cocky, too clever by half. Perhaps I was? More charitably, I was over-sensitive and simply reckless, stung as I had been so often by condescension and being patronised. Envious of highly placed people who could, misguidedly yet seemingly with ease, put their mark on affairs, too often I employed what gifts I had wrongly, tactlessly, to probe for their weak points. What I said at such times may well have been intrinsically accurate – but that could only have made my behaviour all the harder to tolerate!

He stopped in his tracks and I thought he was about to say 'yes'. Obviously he had never asked himself the question. The words red revolution jolted him – too much like calling a spade a bloody shovel. In supporting the Party, enemy of his class and way of life, he was certainly not alone in the phalanx of prominent fellow travellers – Dr Hewlett Johnson, the 'Red Dean' of Canterbury for instance, and John Strachey, that charming but muddled stormy petrel who had been a colleague of Mosley and would soon be a Minister in a Labour government. Like them, in politics at least, Gollancz seemed to cling to the child's conviction that all the nasty things happened to others; after the barricades he too would remain at the top of the heap. Or did he refuse to believe that the Party meant what it said when it talked of *red* revolution?

He stood quite still, head down, then collected himself and said, with a kind of bluster, 'I'm not a Communist! Where did you get that idea from?' He turned to his wife, his voice taking on an anxious note: 'D'you think that's how people see me?' Again she was non-committal. I said the impression he gave, as Pritt did, was that he was as close to the Party as made no matter.

In characteristic fashion he bounced back, turning away from the point. There would be no red revolution in this country. We did not need one because the basic job of class demolition had been accomplished here a long time ago. By the time the war was over we would be on course for socialism by parliamentary means.

If this prophet I had worshipped from afar could be so blind, what hope was there?

Still, his company remained magically stimulating. He presented himself as so enmeshed in the public affairs he commented upon that he spoke from *within* them – the image came to me of a ticker-tape commenting on itself. Publicist to his very marrow, he sniffed the changing wind of ideas shrewdly, if perhaps selectively, in tune with the wartime counterpoint of discussion and controversy, the shifting contemplation of present and future, dizzy juggling with nostrums – initiator and follower, critic and transitory disciple, ideological travelling man.

He discoursed on war aims. As an antidote to war-weariness the manipulators of opinion, himself one of them, had 'sold' people the idea that the war was a price paid for social betterment. Discussion of the nature of that reward would be a useful opiate for the masses! What was wrong with being Machiavellian in a good cause?

In this too he was in tune with the times. People now talked less about how the war was to be won, and far more – amazingly – about the benefits that *should* accrue from having fought it. How could we talk of benefits I wondered?

Surely, I said, there was only *one* aim, to stop the killing and get rid of the fascists? No, he said firmly, that was not enough; the issues had changed. What kind of social order were we to have after the war? We must have better schooling, health care, conditions of living, better social morality – in short, progress towards socialism.

Do you really think, I asked, that we went to war to achieve socialism? He stood his ground; we have to give people a better life to repay them for their sacrifice.

How can you think of *repayment*? Unless, I said, the people at the top feel guilty about getting us into the war? Is it fair to trade on people's sadness and fear of the future simply to get support for you and the Labour Party?

I must have been very disrespectful. When I talked of 'the people at the top', he knew I included *him*, an important leader of opinion in the Thirties, who had helped to create the collective flight from robust action against Fascists and Nazis.

He was patient. I should be more realistic – meaning less naive. This was the way the political game had to be played. The Tories were doing the same! One could do nothing without power. Rab Butler and his friends were cooking up a new deal for education – of course the Tories meant it to be a vote winner! If *they* were already bidding for the post-war vote why shouldn't Labour do so?

That said it all, the whole sad, unscrupulous story of politics – much in my mind at this time. Bernard had urged me to go into politics. He thought I had the mind and the passion for it. Here was the discouraging reality. To be in politics you had to join the power game and become as cynical and opportunist, and as ruthless, as the others. It was a Mephistophelian trap. Principle, where you started from, soon lost its force because, without power, it was futile. You told yourself that principle could be postponed, played down, to *get* power. In the manoeuvres and compromises along the way, principle imperceptibly became secondary, malleable to fit the game, even at times dispensable – until calculations about power, about getting and holding it, excluded all else.

Gollancz expected the Labour Party to find him a seat in Parliament if he wanted one. Could the Labour chiefs, I wondered, having burned their fingers with such as Pritt, afford to have yet another fellow-traveller in the House? I dared not put the question; but he was quick to sense the thought and to forgive it, one of his many engaging qualities. A capricious gleam of sunlight broke through behind the round spectacle lenses, and he grinned boyishly, ruefully, the tooth-brush moustache quivering with mischief. 'After all,' he murmured, 'I *have* done a lot for the Labour cause.'

I doubt if he was convinced that life in the House of Commons would suit him. He had flourished, soared with zest and euphoria, in the freebooting life on the fringes, the fast-moving sharpshooter, uncommitted, untrammelled by party discipline. He must have guessed that the answer might be as I expected, but he would be hurt when it came. There would be no offer of a constituency.

During these talks, Diana's pale, dreamy features contemplated an unknowable infinity. When we were alone she would say: 'The world – what's it got to do with *us*? What we are to each other is all that matters.'

How could that be enough? Confined within four walls and domesticity! Where would the wide world be then? I thought of father's fate. I began to understand, at last, what he had tried to tell me long ago, when I was about fourteen and already working in the factory: that his way forward had been blocked when mother had insisted on joining him in this country too soon, from *der heim*. Her coming had burdened him before he had had a chance, as he put it, 'to do something with myself', to confront the world and taste victory. He blamed himself; he should have stood firm and let her wait. His better nature had betrayed him. The truth was, perhaps, that in letting her come he found a convenient excuse for failure? He had doubted his ability to carry the burdens of family life and still be truly himself, to use his powers to the full; and that doubt had crippled him.

Had he infected me with the same doubt? I knew in my bones that Diana's vision was right. It was there, in the heart, that life should be rooted. But I *would* not see it.

In years to come I would curse myself for a blindness that was close to arrogance. I would then understand – too late – what Peer Gynt meant, the battered seeker returning to his starting point: 'Fool that I was, my empire was *here*!'

But there would be no Solveig waiting for me.

It was not only Diana's vision of things. Others had tried to show it to me: Rachel, Bunty in her siren song in the factory, even perhaps Annie.

In Gollancz I sensed a frightening object lesson. He had conquered much more than I – starting from nothing – could ever hope to, but he had little feeling of triumph. Like the eyes of the Trolls in the Dovre Mountain – always seeing things awry – his vision too had turned away from the heart. Awareness of that neglect, the arid area beneath the flourishing surface, must have come to him in recent years, together with the perception that he lacked the power – or the will – to correct it. In that dispiriting knowledge, aware also, perhaps, that the inner conflict was blunting his touch, once so sure, he had fought doggedly on as before.

Mrs Gollancz, dark-haired and pale, reserved, outwardly serene, had something of Diana's dreamy quality. To my surprise, she invited me to see her collection of Leeds pottery. What, I wondered, went through the mind of this well-intentioned woman, daughter of a rich house, to imagine that her luxury hobby would mean anything to a poor lad from the Gorbals? Diana, I knew, had told them where I came from. Much later, remembering this moment, I would think of John Betjeman, similarly at a loss for a point of contact with me. For Victor, too, the word Gorbals had meant little, simply a remote social fact. For her, it seemed, as for Diana, it must have had no meaning at all.

The very idea of collecting things struck me as strange. Apart from anything else, it meant that one already possessed a sufficiency of all the things one needed!

As she stood before the tall tan-coloured wooden cabinets containing the collection, the pieces gleaming in their still serenity on the shelves, I could almost see some quality in them stretch out to her in sympathy, like hands reaching out to a friend. Showing them, perhaps, may have been her unthinking way of testing young men for suitability, for sympathetic rapport – if they shared her feeling for these objects, they would do? I respected her, and so it was natural for me to admire them for her sake. There was surely more than this? We lingered there in the stillness of the afternoon; from a shelf here and there she took a piece and smoothed her fingertips over its flutings and the entwinings of the handle, and murmured something about it – the words of little importance in themselves. They reached out and sought an answer, but not from me. Somewhere, from far away, she listened to other voices. Incongruously, with a little shiver of shock, I had a vision of Madame Ranevsky looking out of the window and surveying her cherry orchard, soon to be lost. Perhaps, after all, some sympathy did flow between us? Much later I would understand. I must have sensed her premonition, or perhaps a perception slow in its maturing, of changes begun long before – that for her husband the soaring years were over.

The Rip van Winkle feeling was strong, here at the corner of The High and Turl Street. In place of Oxford's earlier sedate pace, the atmosphere of quiet detachment, as if the world began and ended here, there was a sense of volcanic action on the surface and purposeful scheming beneath – all with distant horizons in view. Unending streams of traffic, predominantly military, roared indifferently through. The narrow pavements overflowed with service uniforms – Poles in tilted polygonal caps, Free French in képis, Americans in what seemed the unmilitary garb of draped jackets and pale oyster shaded trousers, British in a variety of unfamiliar regimental and divisional flashes. Strangest of all were the bearded faces and raffishly shapeless khaki – the new, carefree identity of the commandos.

Gowns were few; one suspected that many were guiltily concealed. Students were in the main distinguishable because most of them looked absurdly young – even to me – little more than fresh-faced schoolboys. There seemed to be many more women in the streets than before, their numbers augmented by students from evacuated colleges, Westfield and the Slade, workers from the Cowley motor works, and from the ministries and other governmental or ancillary institutions like Chatham House and the British Council, housed in some of the colleges.

In place of the old ethos of unchallengeable confidence, mannered languor, display of foppish indifference – echoes of Oscar – there was intensity, immediacy, calculation; and over all a cloud of uncertainty.

The Oxford I had left for the army had changed little since that first morning long ago when I rode in on my bike from the Gorbals; it was then still enclosed in its *fin de siècle* dreams and hiding its confusion beneath many masks, listening to the shades of Wilde, Pater, Ruskin, Morris, Hardy, tilting at bourgeois values peevishly and selectively – one suspected somewhat enviously – straining to hear the pure voice of Nature, fearing science and the machine, praising muscle and sinew in lingering loyalty to the arts and crafts movement. The gibe 'arty-crafty' was in vogue, wistfully disowning a faded illusion. I had marvelled at the prevalence of Morris wallpapers and curtains full of freshness and light. In the Gorbals, if walls were covered at all – which was the 'respectable' thing – the paper was in traditional designs of flowered trellises printed in dark colours 'so as not to show the dirt'. In the more progressive North Oxford houses, simplicity, vegetable dyes, pastel shades, rough-textured materials – proclaiming hand-work – in curtains and furnishings and even clothes, were things of faith.

Nearly everyone's rooms had a Van Gogh or Cézanne print. In the Glasgow Art Gallery where I used to make pencil or pastel copies of pictures, I had been under the spell of the Romantics, fascinated by their pastoral and sylvan scenes, dark and full of mystery. Here the innocence of the Impressionists, the stillness, the purity of colour, a new and magical openness, drew the mind deep into the heart of the world, where a long-locked door had been opened to let sunlight and joy and hope flood in. Seeing them everywhere, apparently as necessary as icons to the devout, I was misled. They did not express the feeling of the Thirties, but rather the sunset beliefs and hopes of progressive souls more than half-a-century before, when salvation might lie in retrieving lost links with Nature, and only a touch on the helm was needed to bring the world back on course to rediscover the Golden Age.

———

In my previous life here, standing on this spot beside the pale green wall of the Mitre Hotel, it was still possible to imagine that Bradley's untroubled world of Mr Verdant Green was not so far away – to whom it was said, not entirely in jest, that if he stood in the middle of The High and fired a pistol in any direction he could be fairly certain of not hitting anybody! Now, a tidal wave of people raged past. Going where? With what new thoughts? To what purpose? Ah yes – those questions were now urgent for me too.

In the world of the intellect also, this place had been living in the past, still fascinated, like the eighteenth and nineteenth centuries, by the shifting images of truth and illusion. The logical positivists, acclaimed as innovators in philosophy, wrestled with language, or rather the imprecise use of it – concerned with questions like 'When is a statement a non-statement?' Echoes were heard in the cant nonsense of sherry party talk, as always mordantly accurate in attacking scholarly conceits: 'Have you been to any interesting non-events lately?' or 'Ask me a non-question and I'll give you a non-answer!'

If distinguished and gifted people could not move beyond such trivial exercises, there must be crippling self-doubt in the contemporary culture greater than at any time since the later Middle Ages – a conclusion soon to be confirmed by the vogue acclaim given to the pretentious posturings of the existentialists.

An exception, far from generously recognised, was R. G. Collingwood in his luminous exposition of the proper business of philosophical enquiry, in lectures and in the Olympian sweep of his book *Speculum Mentis*. Its opening sentences I would remember in all the years to come: 'All thought exists for the sake of action. We try to understand ourselves and our world only in order that we may learn how to live.'

This down-to-earth, lucid statement, joining hands across the millenia with Socrates, must have been too challenging and too critical for the Oxford of that epoch. Though *Speculum Mentis* had been published fifteen years before, Collingwood was respected for an earlier work, something quite different, excellent within its scope but offering no such challenge to contemporary thinkers – *Roman Britain*.

Stevenson, at the Institute of Experimental Psychology, a refreshing person who transmitted his enthusiasms with the infectious zest of a questing schoolboy, talked of the pecking order of hens, a line of thought hailed as providing revolutionary insight into the nature of society. Its attraction was demonstrated by its appearance in cant speech: 'Where is So-and-So in the pecking order?' What, I wondered, could differences of status in the animal kingdom tell us about Man that we did not already know? Ideas about the natural heirarchy among people, differing abilities and rank, qualities of leadership, interdependence, were as old as classical Greece. Pecking order theory *might* give comfort, I supposed, to people who were guilty about opposing egalitarianism – for if individuals of other species were not equal within their groupings, why should we expect men and women to be?

Gollancz chided me for being 'too young to be an old conservative'. How *could* I be conservative, I reminded him, coming from where I did? He insisted in his judgment: I had obviously swung too far in the opposite direction. As a product of the Gorbals, he said, I was living proof of the need to correct inequality; how then could I question this article of socialist faith? I mentioned the day, at school, when I came top of the class – so intolerable to the others that it got me the worst beating of my life! Was it my fault if I was so far *unequal*? Should one attempt to 'correct' such an inequality? If you gave the less able person the same status or reward as the high performer, where was the incentive to excel? He refused to see the point; I was, he complained, confusing the issue.

Standing here, noting servicemen's badges of rank, and the bowler hats of senior civil servants, the pecking order was obvious and in full strength. It was not Stevenson's fault that people were so insecure, so burdened with historic anxiety, that they seized on scientific objectivity for solid ground to stand on. Solidity had gone. Among these restless crowds, a new, iconoclastic, opportunist view of life predominated, epitomised in the sardonic barrack-room maxim 'any gravy train will do'.

A new, specifically wartime city – foreign in many senses – superimposed on the old one, hummed with the management of war. Tucked away in back alleys, or in specially erected huts on college playing fields, were organisations rumoured to be 'hush-hush', enclaves of barbed wire.

The aloof world of university licensed lodgings, in its old gentlemanly amplitude of two rooms per person, had shrunk. Hundreds of landladies had doubled and trebled their incomes by converting their houses to bed sitting-rooms. A new, cosy, stifling world of the bed-sitter had taken over; with narrow divan bed, sometimes the luxury of a wash-basin behind a curtain, wheezing gas fire with a little boiling ring to the side of it on a hinged bracket.

This usurping city also housed thousands of refugees of many origins, most of them comfortably off people who had no apparent purpose here but to avoid the London bombing. There was also a sub-world of miscellaneous misfits, exiles stranded in Britain by the war. An example was Domenico Altamura. Son of a rich South American landowning family, he had lived in Britain since childhood, gone to a leading public school, and war had come while he was trying, in leisurely fashion, to complete his education in Oxford. Family remittances reduced by the war, he supplemented them with his wages as a clerk in the Pickles and Sauces Section of the Ministry of Food. He had applied to join the RAF to train as a pilot, but for some obscure reason of diplomatic protocol had been refused entry to any of the services. Behind the patrician nonchalance, he was bitter at being denied the chance to fight for the only country he knew.

He was tall, broad-shouldered, with narrow hips and the balanced poise of the athlete. His long features had a Latin pallor. The black hair brushed back from the temples was unruly and sprang up in little horns; and when in full fig for a Bollinger rout in the old days, in long black cloak lined with flame-red silk, he was perfect for the Mephistophelian role. Laconic, correct, with a sardonic wit, one might imagine that he consciously played the classic upper-class Englishman, but that would have been unfair; he really was that Englishman, in upbringing, education, outlook. The touch of self-mockery marked the spirit of the man, a wry affirmation of his predicament – held by Destiny in a country whose ethos was his, that he was prepared to die for, but which denied him the privilege. Pickles and Sauces, he solemnly explained, were vital to the war effort. Because of meat rationing, the sandwiches that coal miners took down the mine usually contained meat loaf somewhat bland in taste, and in the obscurity often unrecognisable as meat – and so the tang of pickles or sauce reassured them and imparted greater zest for much-needed coal production! His work in Pickles and Sauces, therefore, was crucial for morale. The ironic style was part of his slow, tight-lipped, brooding charm. He was compelled to explain away – weakly, comically, as he well knew – a status far below his aristocratic vision of himself. In his case, he thus insisted, there was clearly a fault in the pecking order.

There were deserters from the services. Hubert, of distinguished family, as an undergraduate had been a model of the Regency buck; from the army he had returned in a new avatar as aesthete and anarchist, and lived in a rotting old shed, rat-infested, on the canal bank near the slum area of Jericho. Dapper, with mockery in the cold blue eyes, the ruddy features showed early intimations of the brighter scarlet of the hardened toper. He composed poetry, played the flute, and wrote letters to the newspapers about the futility of war. He seemed to take no pains to conceal his fugitive position; obviously, money enabled him to live outside the system, or rather to make it 'work' his way. A deserter lacking money, and forced to get a job without the appropriate documents, would put himself in someone's power. I never discovered how Hubert managed without a ration book for food and clothing coupons. One could eat tolerably – for about ninepence – at the subsidised British Restaurant in George Street without producing a ration book. To buy food in the shops, however, would mean dealing in the black economy. With aristocratic detachment, like Bakunin, Hubert saw no contradiction between anarch- ist principles and the use of wealth to live well by manipulating the system. I thought again of Jimmy Robinson, diehard anarchist, doing well by making the system 'pay', as he put it, while fighting it at the same time. Hubert, Jimmy, Gollancz – strange bedfellows!

Domenico and Hubert, as far as I knew, never met. Essentially from the same social class, the war had put them in different worlds. Hubert had defected to join the shadowy, bohemian one – the term 'drop-out' was not yet current – of those who by temperament or tradition were ranged against conventional society. Domenico, on a different fringe, supporting his straitened circumstances with aristocratic panache, stood unquestioningly for established values. Had he met Hubert and dis- covered he was a deserter, he would have seen it as his Englishman's duty to denounce him.

Possibly someone did denounce him; or he may have run his luck too far. One day, as I stood looking at the display of books in Blackwell's windows, he came up and prodded me in the ribs. Unusually, he wore a gown over the shabby army jacket. Ruddy features flushed, he bubbled over with excitement, part hilarious, part serious: 'Guess what! I've just been progged!' (caught in a misdemeanour by the Proctors). The commonest reason was being discovered in an out-of-bounds pub. Being a deserter, in effect an outlaw, this was a bizarre stroke of ill-fortune.

On being challenged, he must have given his true name and college. He may have done so because, in liquor, he was off-guard, or it may have been an automatic expression of upper-class arrogance. More likely, tired of living in the shadows, he had unconsciously put himself in the way of being caught – accidentally on purpose? I wondered what to say; from the eager look on his face he expected me to share his hysterical mood. It was customary to commiserate with someone for such bad luck – apart from being fined there could be considerable inconvenience – but I had for some time resented his mixture of boss class condescension and his charade of living as a deprived member of the working class. He lived in the lower depths *from choice*, not necessity. Being progged served him right! Still, it would have been unkind to say so. Before I could think of an acceptable remark, he waved a hand to dismiss me as a dullard, and rushed off up the Broad, presumably in search of someone more responsive, his gown streaming defiantly behind him. Later I heard that he had disappeared from Oxford. Long afterwards I would see his name in the casualty lists and think of him sadly, with compassion, a rare, unfortunate soul – who had been, for reasons totally different from mine, equally lonely.

Domenico and Hubert represented two aimless groupings in suspense. Other, purposeful ones, were hard at work. In this frenetic city, so closely linked to the *realpolitik* of the war, one sensed the muffled clamour of people plotting to reshape the future to their designs, manipulating whatever forces they could – a microcosm of the world in apocalypse. Nothing was still. The worlds of political intrigue, personal manoeuvre, and fleeting passion interflowed. In tall Victorian houses among the North Oxford evergreens, in cramped bed-sitters in Walton Street, in college rooms, even in the streets and pubs, there was volatile talk, groups and pairs drawing aside from the stream, interchanging and reforming as in a classic dance – molten sympathy and scheming. Hectic, tumid excitement fed on instant intimacy and instant confidences, a hunger to fill each moment with the whole of life.

Some groups, especially those linked to governments in exile, plotted for advantage in their countries after the war; others, without nominal statehood, lobbied in the corridors of Allied power to turn promises or rhetoric into commitment. In a Zionist circle, a leading spirit was Walter Ettinghausen, a don at Queen's, a stocky figure with high bulging forehead; a man of charm, force of character, and sense of mission.

Walter Ettinghausen's confidence was strong; he may have had better grounds for it than most, possibly through contacts in the shadowy international bargaining. In the event, he would go to Palestine immediately after the war, and as Walter Eytan achieve high position in Israel, as Director-General of the Ministry for Foreign Affairs and Ambassador to France. The change of name, common among the first pathfinders, would perhaps be prompted in his case partly by the desire to shed the German associations of Ettinghausen – born in Munich in 1910, he went to St Paul's School and Oxford – partly by the compulsion to make a declamatory gesture. 'Eytan', a Hebrew word meaning strength or immovability, in this case would stand for 'indomitable, unconquerable', but with Old Testament overtones too, for instance in reference to the 'original strength' of the Patriarchs. In retrospect the choice of name, apart from offering intriguing insight into the man's vision of himself, and more to the point how he *wanted* to be seen – revealed a great deal about the ethos that possessed the builders of the new state.

Ettinghausen was a fine chess player, and it was chess that first drew me into the circle. I learned the game on my first landfall here, and was now rated a strong player. Chess, however, was not the circle's primary interest, which was to create a Jewish state in Palestine after the war. That, for most of us, remained fanciful, a mirage in the desert. Still, perhaps because so much else was in the melting pot, there was a feeling in the air, inexplicably, that history might decide, in this at least, to favour the dreamers.

In Ettinghausen's circle I met some of the group I had seen riding down the Broad singing *Hatikvah* long ago. Hannah, working at Bletchley Park – 'writing reports' was all she would say of her duties – was sometimes there, her willowy form elegantly turned out in finely tailored tweeds and sheer nylons, then as rare as peacocks' feathers. Her fair hair, once worn in long ringlets, was now cut short, and the curls nestled round the translucent features, emphasising their firm moulding and the pensive set of the lips – a Judith awaiting her heroic hour. Thoughts of Rachel drew us together.

I ran into Werner there, and that was something of a shock. Not having seen or heard from him for over two years, I had assumed that the break had been deliberate. He had vanished from Oxford from one day to the next, and no one knew, or would say, where he had gone. Only later did I hear that he had been interned. In those far off 'last days' – as I thought of them – people did simply slip quietly away. Even so, I had been hurt to find that he had left without a message of any kind. In fact, he said, he *had* written a few lines, which the authorities told him would be sent to me. If that note *was* written, it never reached me. Presumably, as an enemy alien, any message he wrote was suspect, and this one may have got no further than some confidential file. Absorbed with my imminent departure to the war – and, as I thought, to death – tracing him was beyond me. From the army, I wrote to him several times care of his Oxford research institute. Getting no reply, I said to myself 'Put it down to experience!' – one of Bernard's favourite comments on life's disappointments.

He told me that he had written to me many times from the internment camp, and afterwards too – presumably when I was still in the army – and had been desolated by my silence.

Even in the Gorbals, I reflected, where the emotional language was familiar, signals had sometimes been hard to read – and to trust. In Oxford, learning a new code, I had often misread a comment or action as a slight and turned away, and discovered, sometimes too late to remedy, that people found me aloof, difficult to get to know. Now, after another type of isolation in the army, I had to learn to read the signs anew. In time, I would conclude that Werner *had* written. Buchenwald and the rest had broken his patrician detachment. In the Isle of Man, he told me later, puzzling over my silence, reassessing me over and over again, he had reminded himself that I had always been dependable, never once asked him for anything; he could talk to me from the heart and I would say what I thought, holding nothing back. He had missed that solidity.

Which of us, I wondered, was the less mature *now* – which the smaller man! Many years senior, he should have been stronger, more thoughtful than this? It was time I ceased to assume that others were always the more mature – wiser in the world, more competent. Why did it not occur to him, for instance, that some mishap had befallen *me*? Back in Oxford, he could easily have found out that I was in the army – and speculated about my fate?

Slowly, in this strange, wary, buccaneering city, we moved towards a kind of trust once again.

As for our missing letters, it occurred to us that the answer might lie in his secret work and the accompanying surveillance upon him. He never did tell me what the work was. His correspondence, inwards and outwards, must have been intercepted, and some of it withheld. But why should *my* letters have been stopped? By an extraordinary chance I was to stumble on a possible answer. I met a girl who worked in one of the intelligence sections at Blenheim. In her bed-sitter one evening, as we sat in a tipsy huddle close to the wheezing gas fire, she murmured that she had seen my unusual name in an index of Communists. Her hand flew to her mouth in shock at what she had revealed, and quickly, as camouflage, she converted her guilt into concern for me: 'You *must* be careful! – though it's surely some silly mistake to have your name there at all. *You* don't talk like a Communist!'

Had there been a time when I *had* talked like one? The entry, I supposed, must date from the days when Bernard was a leading Party member – and I had been branded red by association? That, perhaps, made me an unsatisfactory person – a bad risk – for Werner to correspond with?

I would never be able to tell him this without revealing the source. I kept her secret.

Only at this chance meeting at Ettinghausen's did I learn that Werner's wife and children had been killed. 'I am not superstitious,' he said, 'at least I try not to be. It seemed the right decision, at the time, to stay on here. If I had gone to America when I intended, they would still be alive. Ah yes – if!' He raised his hands and let them fall back on his knees.

Werner was thinner now. The sleek black hair, brushed tightly back from the domed brow, had receded further; in the long, pointed features the mouth was tighter, the lines beside it deeper. I had to look carefully to discern the shadow of the once debonair *flâneur* I had first met, a lifetime away, in distant green days.

I wondered if he had thought back, in guilt, to the philandering that had so shocked Rachel. Astonishingly, he did know what she had thought about him. Gently, kindly, she had begged him to mend his ways. As he told me of it, her voice spoke to me out of the darkness. Oh Rachel – sincere and forthright spirit, seeing all things simply! In this instance too she had spoken wisely, and in vain. Now, when Werner scourged himself for the fate of his wife and children, it was for his error of judgment, nothing more.

What of me? If I had listened to her, she too might still be alive?

He talked on, meditating on her words. 'What I was doing, she said, might bring a judgment on me. What a woman! She spoke from a good heart. But I am a scientist. I think logically. Did the German bombers *know* that I had been playing about with women and therefore decide to drop the bomb at precisely that moment?' He shrugged. 'Those little affairs had no world-shaking meaning! I *like* women! – flirting as you say? No it is more than flirting; a little diversion here and there – innocent pleasure! After it you go on your way with no harm done. What is it but a natural expression of the masculine personality – what Freud calls the libido? – a different motive entirely from marriage? Women are so insecure about such things. They refuse to understand!'

Half-bitterly, half-whistling in the dark, he referred to himself as a 'reconstituted' bachelor. Reconstituted was a wartime word everybody had had to learn – reconstituted dried eggs, dried milk, dried baby-food . . . He pursued the role with slowly returning zest. His flat in St Giles, not far from the Lamb and Flag pub, became a convivial place, destined to live in my memory for many reasons, pleasure and friendship, and self-knowledge – not always pleasurable, especially in a grotesque experience, which I explain in its place later, when I would put myself in danger of killing a man or being killed, a hero for no good reason: and I would discover for myself that fear, as Bernard had said, did not strike at the moment of its genesis; you simply acted, did what you were impelled to do, and then the fear would surge home overwhelmingly, shocking reminder of brooding death, and return again and again over the years.

On most Saturday nights Werner threw a party that stretched well over into the Sunday. The flat was usually well-stocked with liquor and food, mainly from the black market, but it was understood that guests brought what food and drink they could; judging by the quantity and quality thus donated – good champagne, smoked salmon, fine chocolate, even caviare sometimes – most of it came from privileged sources, the services or diplomatic missions. This life, insouciant in spite of the *angst* of war – or perhaps because of it – suited him. After the war, he thought, he would probably stay on in Oxford; plenty of young women, sport, parties, convenient for the bright lights of London – why not?

'Even if the Zionist dream does come true,' he said, 'I am not the pioneer type; but it *will* not, that is sure! No one will give the Jews anything.

Apart from that I am not cut out to be a conspirator either. In any case I must keep my nose clean, as they say. I have had blows enough to last me all my life. I do not want to be sent back to the Isle of Man as an unreliable alien.'

In this rough, jostling foreign city, unsettling reminders of *realpolitik* and its tireless scheming constantly appeared. I went to Chatham House with the idea of earning some extra money translating from German newspapers; abortively as it turned out because, worried about accuracy, and steeped as I was in the High German of the classics and Fraulein Wüschak's mandarin style, I was too slow at turning colloquial German into English. That glimpse behind the scenes of war, however, was disturbing. From here, though it was not the only source, government departments, and presumably the intelligence services, were provided with foreign press summaries. This output would influence policy analysis and strategic judgment – what the enemy wanted its peoples to know, or indirectly the world at large; what was being concealed and what the concealment itself indicated, and conversely, why certain things *were* selected to be known. What, on the other hand, should *we* feed into the great Byzantine shadow play? The end result? Redesigned strategy perhaps, adjusted tactics possibly, death and destruction none the less. Yet everything looked so harmless! In these dingy college rooms whose grimy leaded windows, criss-crossed with sticky tape against bomb blast, kept out more light than they let in, charming, cultivated people sat among piles of newsprint, drinking tea and reading the papers – as if at a marathon March Hare breakfast – pausing now and then to send reports over the wires or by courier. Similar people did likewise in Germany and in many other countries. What price the noble fourth estate, supposed instrument of enlightenment, used for deception, invasion of the mind, thought control!

The newspapers and magazines were fresh. Obviously most of the enemy material was flown in from neutral countries, but a macabre fantasy struck me – the war was being *co-operatively* organised between the obliging combatants – reminding me of the story featured in the 'Nicht wieder Kreig' exhibition in Glasgow, of the factory on the border between France and Germany that had supplied munitions to both sides in the First War; the inference being that the combatants co-operated to keep that supply line open for each other.

Someone tapped me on the shoulder: 'Contemplating the eternal verities eh?' Bill Challoner stood beside me on the narrow pavement, leaning on his heavy stick. His features were less drawn than when I had met him on the river path a few weeks before. The long khaki greatcoat was creased as though he had slept in it, but worn this time draped over the shoulders like a cloak. The badges of rank were gone from the epaulets, but little black holes showed where the major's crowns had been. The well-cut double-breasted suit of chalk-stripe clerical grey, to my experienced eye new, also betrayed itself as having been tailored for someone with influence, or money; the trousers had turn-ups, forbidden by the clothes rationing regulations – another sign of high status in the pecking order!

The man with him was somewhat older, in his thirties, also in civilian clothes, dark, dapper, keen-eyed, intense. He reminded me of Bernard in his pre-disillusion days. Introducing him, Bill called him Colonel, indicating – not only by the formal address but the tone of voice – that he was in some way of importance to him. Oxford seemed full of surprisingly young majors and half-colonels – eager *apparatchiks*, able, ruthless, glorifying in virtuoso manoeuvre. I will call him Colonel James. Both of them looked flushed, and James was unsteady on his feet.

'We're just going to have tea.' Bill indicated the Mitre Hotel at our backs. 'Come and join us?'

James had the trick of regarding you with head inclined, scrutinising you warily beneath the lowered brow, partly concealing his expression. As we turned towards the Mitre, he seemed to stoop still further, lost his balance and would have fallen on his face if Bill had not caught him by the arm and hauled him erect. One of Bill's nicknames was Stone Head; he was one of those rare drinkers who showed little outward sign of the effects. He murmured to me that they had just come from a rather heavy lunch. It was getting on for five in the afternoon. He looked at me steadily, rubbing the side of his nose with a forefinger. I caught the warning and did not ask where. The word 'heavy' obviously referred to more than drink; he and James had been in attendance, as staff officers, at a high-level meeting.

In the low-ceilinged lounge, dark panelled, the broad sash windows, their sills at knee height, were tightly closed to exclude the noise of the High, as they had shut the world out for generations. The leather in the old brass-studded chairs was cracked with age, and perhaps wartime ill-use; the ceiling was yellow with old smoke. In the dimness of the late afternoon, a breath of sadness rose up from the red patterned carpet and squat oaken tables, a sense of faded, invaded dignity. The tubby white-haired waiter, in a shiny black suit, was much as I remembered him from the 'last days', as was the great tea tray with brass handles, but not its austere fare or furnishings – a square china pot of weak tea, thick cups and saucers instead of fine Wedgwood, a metal jug for milk, a chipped china rack with triangles of tired toast, a little dish with three small blobs of margarine and another with a few teaspoonfuls of thin jam. James, who had flown in the previous day from the fleshpots of Washington, inspected the tray and sighed.

He and Bill were obviously still borne up by the excitement of momentous discussions at lunch. I did not know at the time that the meeting – at a country house not far from Oxford – had concerned Operation Overlord, and the position of de Gaulle. Left to themselves they might have been tempted to exchange thoughts about it, which Bill must have been desperate to avoid for fear of being overheard; hence his decision to shepherd James about in the noise of the streets, where eavesdropping was less likely, until, sobered up, he could safely see him on his way. Having spotted me at the corner, Bill had watched me for some minutes, to be sure I was not waiting to meet someone; I could guess the rest. The pain in his bad leg had become unbearable from trudging about; at all costs he must sit down. He hit upon the idea of getting me to join them, in the hope that in the presence of a stranger James's training would assert itself and keep his tongue under control. As far as I could guess, the gamble succeeded, but only just.

Even so, James's efforts to control his tongue were pathetically obvious. Restlessly he glanced about the empty room, tugged at his lower lip, stared at Bill as though pleading for a safe cue. Though Bill looked the more composed, almost his normal self, they both talked excitedly, compulsively, as one might when a subject uppermost in the mind threatens to burst out, hoping that a torrent of extraneous talk would block the dangerous channel. As always, the forbidden subject must have exercised a powerful, spiteful magnetism. Not surprisingly it occurred to me – since here were two staff officers who, I guessed, were close to great affairs – that the secret concerned what everyone suspected was in train, the plan for an Allied 'return' to Europe. Whatever it was, their desperately irrelevant talk must have skirted the censored subject closely.

James, service aide to a ministerial committee dealing with de Gaulle, grumbled about the incessant difficulties created by the proud, spiky general.

'Why do you put up with him?' I asked. 'You people put him there! You can stop backing him if he's hampering the war effort?'

'It's too late. Whether we like it or not, whatever he was before, he is now *the* Free French leader.'

Immediately after the fall of France, when it was crucial to find someone to personify France in exile and command its forces, James had worked for a steering group in the anxious governmental discussions as to whom Britain should support for that role. It was vital that a clearly dominant leader should emerge quickly. In some ways, James mused tipsily, he himself had been a lucky man – in the right place at the historic moment; his canny, astute voice, at a time of such uncertainty, might have tipped the delicate balance in favour of de Gaulle. At one stage General Giraud seemed a possibility. Another was Admiral Darlan, the intransigent commander who had resisted British proposals, after the surrender on the mainland, that French naval units should be placed under British control. A powerful figure, the object of considerable French loyalty, it was feared that Darlan wanted to set up a new sovereign entity, based on French colonial territories, and break free of the Alliance. There was also a suspicion that he might use his control of still formidable French sea power to bargain with the Germans. Britain dared not risk such a 'third force' on its flanks. I remarked that at the time I myself had thought that this deadly danger clamoured for a classic Byzantine solution, assassination. Just as I was later to pray that Hitler might invade Russia, and wake to find the prayer answered, amazingly Darlan *was* assassinated. Yes, James casually said, it was no accident. There was no other way.

'Of course,' he went on enthusiastically, 'we were right to plump for de Gaulle' – meaning that *he* had been right.

'How can you tell if he *is* the right man,' I wondered aloud. 'The French people have no say in the matter? Obviously, whoever has the backing of the Allies will be the 'sitting tenant' when the war is over, and he will step straight into the Elysée Palace. The French will be saddled with de Gaulle for a long time, whether they like it or not. You people have made the choice for them.'

'But he's so obviously successful,' James began, then stopped, glancing at Bill, who looked away.

'How can he *not* be successful?' I persisted. 'There's no one to measure him against! You, a few strategically placed individuals, have fixed the nature of France after the war – you've determined the history of France, the history of Europe, for the next – what? – fifty years? He nodded excitedly, savouring the thought. The war had given him, fleetingly, a spell at the wheel of Destiny.

So this was how the world lurched through 'time and chance'? People like James and Bill, brilliant, artful schemers behind the scenes of an apocalyptic puppet show, ventriloquists speaking through the mouths of the seeming holders of power? Was the whole of life, the 'great sweep of history', as empty of principle as this – the world run by grown-up school prefects, descendants of Stalky & Co., with cleverness, power of persuasion, nudging the figureheads this way and that?

Bill had been studying me gravely. 'You should go into politics,' he said. 'You're too fundamental for the likes of us. *We* are just the operators behind the scenes! We enjoy the game, that's all. We have no principles really, except to keep the *status quo* – the game as we know it. We know the ropes. We're not interested in anything else.'

He was speaking, typically, with Machiavellian false modesty. He meant that he and James and their like would always be the true prime movers behind the scenes – *eminences grises*, who would implacably retain the decisive power.

Yes: they would always be the fixers, the cool-headed operators, the secretive network of power that I would never be permitted to join. They sensed, finely tuned as they were, that I was not cut out for the role. They and their circle *might* just conceivably allow me a minor one – even pay tribute, when it suited them, to my high principles – permitting me a small amount of influence, until the time came for me to be displaced, or neutralised, when I ceased to serve 'the game'.

Guessing my thoughts, he murmured, 'That's the way the world wags, old boy. The pecking order works in mysterious ways!'

He smiled to himself, and nodded thoughtfully.

13

Figures in a Breughel Landscape

In vino veritas applies in behaviour as well as in speech. One summer night, so drunk that I had to cling to the nearest wall to stay upright, I left a party in Beaumont Street on my way to another in Museum Street. The night was balmy and still. A great round moon hung in the luminous sky; and in its light the simple domestic façades, flint-grey, with transomed doorways and window embrasures and glazing bars picked out in white, stood out in muted silvery splendour against the dark velvet background of the night. The street was deserted, or so it appeared, enclosed as I was in alcohol's special isolation. To me it was entirely normal to be moving along hand over hand against the walls, floating through this breathless world as Cocteau would portray Orpheus making his way through a silent Hades in his film *Orphée*. Nearing the corner where Beaumont Street gave way to the wide expanse of St Giles – the Giler – the rusticated stonework of the Ashmolean Museum's screen wall comfortingly rough to the touch, the grey pinnacles of the Martyrs' Memorial some fifty yards away receded and merged into the trees of St Mary Magdalen churchyard behind, seen now in miniature as from the wrong end of a telescope; and Balliol, on the other side of the Giler, squat and muddy in the moonlight, retreated swiftly too and was soon a mile away at least. I clung to the Ashmolean's corner stone, and with the crystal-clear logic of the very drunk, assessed my situation. Of one thing I was sure; I could not cross that immense open space of the Giler on my own two feet. And then, simplicity itself, the solution was obvious – I would crawl across on hands and knees.

In retrospect it is hard to believe that I ignored the cars going past. Some part of me must have dismissed them as irrelevant. Hands and body pressed against the rough stone, I subsided on to my knees and then, reassuringly solid on all fours, made my way over the wide pavement, across the cobble stones of the broad sunken gutter, and steadily – pleased with my cleverness – crawled across the broad roadway, from time to time surprised to see floating lights moving near, like large glow-worms – later realised to have been headlights – approach and float past me, first from my right going left, then from my left going away to my right. At last my hands felt the smooth round cobbles in the gutter on the far side, then the uneven flagstones of the upward incline towards Balliol doors, closed at this hour. Reaching the arched doorway, I pressed against the pitted stonework and climbed up on to my feet; and continued my progress, in the blissful floating manner of hand-over-hand against the walls, aware of nothing but the eerie joy of this primitive victory, and passed along the perimeter walls of Balliol and St John's, turned right through the tunnel entrance to Lamb and Flag Passage to reach the old-world enclave of Museum Street and its single short row of narrow houses, unlit windows open to the soft summer air, and join in the sweet abandon of the night, bottles and glasses passing to and fro, talk and happiness flowing.

The next day at breakfast, casually mentioning the manner of my crossing The Giler, I met a shocked silence, and then: 'Good Heavens – what about the *cars*?' I was about to say that I could not remember any, and then I thought of those lights floating past my head.

Freud says 'What was predictable, was intended', but it is an ancient truth. The drunken mind – or the overwrought one – releases the troubled spirit to cry havoc and trip you up. Perplexed as I was by Sibyline warnings – 'you are on the wrong road, in the wrong place in the wrong epoch!' – perhaps I had asked myself, as father in bitterness must often have done, 'What does it matter if I do destroy myself?'

Yet that day had brought such a bright message, a victory I had told myself I must not expect – as I had also reminded myself when entering for the scholarship. I had sat the examination for the Economics and Political Science Diploma, and that morning I had gone to look at the results newly posted up in the Examination Schools. In the evening I had arranged to meet some of the other candidates – whatever the results – for a classic celebration, and drink the world away. On my way to the Schools I tried to stroll jauntily, to affect a happy indifference, but I must have looked as I felt, wooden, fearful. Again and again I said to myself, falling back upon the old Gorbals sympathetic magic, 'Expect the worst and you won't be disappointed!' How I wished I had not promised to join the revel that evening.

Nearing the Schools, some of the others, returning from their scrutiny of the lists, hailed me with the thumbs-up sign. Thinking they referred to their own results, I tried to look happy for them. At the great dark doors I paused, half-unwilling to go further; the shadowy, cavernous hall, emptied of the rows of examination desks, yawned its indifference. At last I went in. The stone floor chilled the still air. To the left, in deep shadow, on a neo-gothic screen of massive timber, hung the green baize notice board, and pinned on it were the Diploma results in tiny black handwriting. Perversely my eyes went first to the bottom of the sheet of paper, in case I was among those who had not 'satisfied the Examiners'. Slowly I read upwards through the names of those who *had*. My name was not there – anywhere! I turned away and stared again into the brooding shadows of the hall – glad that I stood there alone – and tried to tell myself that it did not matter. I had soared too high. The confident expectations of my tutors here had proved wrong. The gods had spoken. What a sorry mistake to have come to Oxford!

No! Wait! Fury took hold of me, and in that instant I could have torn down the whole world. How could my name not be there? I must *exist*! I turned back to the board as if I would force my name to appear on the paper in letters of flame – Orpheus on Phlegethon. And then, as I stared, I felt cold sweat. In the dimness I had missed – how could I have done! – a few lines of crabbed writing at the very top of the paper, separated from those below by a blank space and a thick black line. Under a heading 'The following were judged worthy of Distinction', were three names; mine was there.

The breakfast table wondered, delicately, not in so many words but plainly enough, how strange it was, on a day of success, to go and put yourself in the way of death, accidentally on purpose. You were lucky this time – one day you won't be!

What I had done was out of character – or so I thought. What was that *alter ego* trying to tell me? Why did success unnerve me so?

The insouciant life here, especially in the first period, before going into the army, was so bewitching that sometimes, awakening in the night, it was hard to believe that I was the person for whom, so recently, the unrelenting burden of work in the noise and steam and squalor of the factory, from dark in the morning till dark at night, had been the natural order of things, and who now dispensed my hours as I pleased – sailing, tennis, squash, the theatre, concerts, parties, sometimes getting drunk; I had never had a drink in my life till I came to Oxford, except for the occasional sip of wine at religious ceremonies. What people here called 'work', reading, essay writing, was pleasure! I touched the hard calloused skin on the palms of my hands. It was true and not true:

> 'Which of us commands here,
> Within this husk of life?
> Which of us will arrive at any destination?
> But if all is conditional,
> Until the final trump,
> Does it matter?'

Instinct made me an indefatigable joiner, participator, explorer of this new world – a flowering unimaginable in the Gorbals days. This appetite was natural enough in a very young man; there were, however, equivocal voices within. A black cloud hid behind the sun, fleetingly appearing and sliding away again, tantalising – reminder and warning. To live this *dolce far niente* existence, beguiled for ever by the Sirens, was surely not the real me? It must surely be a self-indulgent deviation from my true course – if I could only divine what that was. A bout of heightened pleasure would sometimes carry a sting of guilt in its tail – perhaps the residual influence of Calvin and Moses, the powerful mixture permeating the life of the Gorbals. More prosaically, perhaps, the feeling sprang from a sense of living on borrowed time. Unlike most other students here, I could never expect to live in this fashion again.

Sometimes a fog of unease and discontent descended, like the heaviness of the spirit on a 'morning after', but unattributable to any cause. This was a new unease, far more profound than the passing discomfitures of my first days here. Life then, apart from those initial shocks, had had the magical quality of a continuous, wondrous party. Like le Grand Meaulnes I had floated through an enchanted demesne, searching the light and shade of self-discovery and discovery in others, the hours sparkling and short, too short.

Disquiet flowed not only from disillusion, imperceptibly growing. Certainly the distant gleam of Mr Lipchinsky's torch had all but disappeared. A more immediate reason for unease, and guilt, was loneliness. Thinking of it dispassionately, the idea was absurd. I knew dozens of people, to drink and talk with, join for squash or tennis; girls to take to the theatre or concerts or on the river. Yet it was true. I was lonely. Only on Bernard's occasional visits did I speak in a shared idiom. Yes, Alec had been right!

In retrospect, guilt – or was it self-doubt? – showed itself in dramatic, comic, frightening ways, pulling me up short for no obvious reason, awareness of brooding shadows, intimations of Sibylline prophecies wafted away on the wind, to be understood only long afterwards, mostly too late.

At a party in Werner's flat, I took a mortal risk seemingly with a clear head, for I was not drunk, and the danger was plain; I did it, amazed at myself, unhesitatingly.

It was a large party, drawn from a wide spectrum, Bletchley Park and Blenheim, the Slade, university luminaries, service officers – including Bill Challoner and James – and fringe people, self-evacuees seemingly with no greater reason to live in Oxford than anywhere else. Diana and Hannah were there. Bernard was there too; on one of his trips south, he had taken a week-end off to visit me, and Werner, who had warmed to him after their first, somewhat combative meeting on the river bank, had asked me to bring him.

One of the fringe people was Julian, son of an old colonial trading family, a convivial character to be seen most days – depending on the hour – propping up the bar at the Randolph or the Playhouse. Tall, thin, angular, with sharp features drawn tight, sunken eyes glittering with intensity, signs of his condition perhaps; he was tubercular, but I did not know it at the time. Rejected for military service, his surface roughness – probably cultivated – may have sprung from a sense of inadequacy, an unhappy protest at the unfairness of life; brothers and many relatives were in the services, and here he was letting the side down. With a thin moustache and a peremptory way of speaking, he may have hoped to be mistaken for the tight-lipped, dashing officer of his imagination, who just happened to be in civilian clothes. Not far beneath the surface lurked a meditative, solitary soul, attributes that may have helped to bring about the incident.

Another factor, perhaps the crucial one, must have been the undercurrent of homosexuality in this milieu; and it is hard to believe that in my innocence I was unaware of it. I had heard of homosexuality only as a distant, hidden phenomenon, living in the shadows somewhere, which a 'normal' man would be unlikely to encounter. I had had no reason, as far as I knew, to think about it till that evening, still less to speculate about who might be, as Proust put it concerning the Baron de Charlus, 'so'. It would be a long time before I realised how numerous they were, and how unconcernedly their sexual preference was looked upon by these boss class people. The subject hardly ever seemed to crop up in conversation. In fact it did, often, but I had been too green to perceive it – in remarks, for example, about mutual acquaintances and their 'difficult relationship' such as might be made about a fellow and his girl, puzzling because the reference was to two *men*. In the Gorbals, all I had known of homosexuals came from the usual gross stories, so hard to believe. How could love, inseparable from the magic of a woman's silken flesh, exist between men? Homosexuals were thought of as less than manly – the demotic use of the word 'pansy' conveying effeminacy, the opposite of aggressive, muscular, masculinity, the only proper kind. For a 'normal' man to be approached – made a pass at – by a pansy was a terrible affront to which the proper response must be violence, incontrovertible proof that he was not 'so'.

Werner's flat occupied the first floor of an old, rambling building. In its spacious drawing room a low latticed window looked out, through a screen of trees, to the wide expanse of St Giles. A large study opened off it, where, at a long oak refectory table, he would sit his guests when he gave one of his small dinner parties. On the other side of a dark hallway were two big bedrooms, a bathroom and a kitchen. The party flowed over the whole area, into corners, into the shadows of the hall. On the dining table in the study stood rank upon rank of bottles, a whole world of drink, added to as people arrived with their offerings until, space exhausted, new additions formed ranks on the floor below it. They would not stay down there long – these were days of *angst* and thirst. Large serving plates were piled with food, a gourmand's dream come true, denying austerity – smoked salmon, cold meats, cheeses, fruit, biscuits, fine chocolates straight from Washington. Werner, not a great drinker, moved hospitably among his guests refilling glasses.

The party had been in being for about an hour, and some of the early arrivals, going on to dinner, said their good-byes. With their departure, the initial throng, so dense that it was virtually a solid, heaving, clamorous mass, enclosed in a blue fog of cigarette smoke, had thinned into dispersed groups, opening up a clear view through the drawing room doorway to

the rooms on the far side of the hall. I was on the edge of a group standing near the long window, which included Nevill Coghill and Maurice
Bowra; the talk was about a production of *Salômé*. Bowra, next to me,
his interest obviously fading, turned as if to go, brushing against
me; seeming to lose his balance and to save himself he threw an arm
round my hips: 'Dear boy – so sorry!' He righted himself rather slowly,
looking at me fixedly, searchingly. I moved away to break the contact. He
did not look drunk. I must have scrutinised him coldly, the wrong
response presumably. He tried again: 'We've met? At Lindsay's, was it
not?'

To be remembered by an important man was flattering, and I
must have shown that I was pleased, but perhaps not in the right way,
for he stood back, his broad face assuming a distant look of preoccu-
pation, and with an indistinct murmur he turned on his heel and strode
away.

I had had a couple of glasses of champagne, but I was far from drunk.
As he turned away, his expression had been a mixture of annoyance and
hurt. Puzzled I watched him cross the hall and merge with the crowd in
one of the rooms on the far side. What had I done to offend him? It was
beyond me. As I stood, for the moment separate from Coghill and the
others, speculating on the encounter, Bill Challoner came up, leaning
unsteadily on his stick, glass in hand: 'Maurice must be hard up!' he
muttered in my ear. 'I shouldn't have thought you were his type.' So that
was it! Seeing my shock – and resentment – he added quickly: 'My dear
chap it's nothing – really it isn't. It's par for the course!' Then with a tilt
of the head he indicated Hannah and Diana at the door talking to
Bernard; Hannah's willowy form leaned on the door frame, her hip
curving out, breathtakingly defined in the straight grey skirt. 'In any case
you're doing all right!' His wolfish grin was eloquent – there, surely, is
living proof that you are not 'so'!

If Bill was right, and this *had* been a pass, was there something about
me, an unconscious mannerism, that misled some people into thinking I
was 'so'? Paradoxically, I was glad that I had *not* understood, for the
ingrained Gorbals reaction would have been to knock the fellow down –
a matter of honour; and where would that have landed me! Bill, in his
kind, intuitive fashion, was comforting me – the pass was nothing to be
upset about.

———

His words prompted a different worry, however, in its way much more important; I had failed once again to read the infernal code of this place. I cursed myself for a fool. I should have known – of course I should. What Bill had called 'par for the course', must happen to all of them, and some must welcome it. For all I knew, such passes had been made at me before and I simply had not noticed. Bill leaned close again: 'One doesn't mention these things. I'm doing so because you look a trifle puzzled.' He meant *upset* but was too nice to say so. 'He's not a bad sort actually. As a matter of fact, he's not my type either!'

These words, too, startled me, or at least the Gorbals part of me with its stereotype of the pansy as effeminate; for Bill fitted to perfection the standard image of the tough, masculine man. He was also very much the ladies' man. That term, I reflected, had its own germane ambiguities, implying, among other things, that some men were – in the 'wrong' sense – men's men! That too was par for the course. It was not done to notice it, least of all to comment upon it.

I saw Bowra emerge from the far room and look about him tight-lipped. Werner was moving through the hall dispensing champagne. Bowra went up to him, a rigid smile suddenly donned like a mask, spoke briefly, nodded a brisk farewell and hurried out of the front door. In a few moments, glancing out of the window, I saw him stride through the line of trees and cross St Giles.

What, I wondered, would have been the right way to deal with the pass? – that is, one that would not have led to the man's obvious ill-humour? Perhaps there *was* no such way? Something in Bill's manner, even his words 'par for the course', suggested that for most young men of his class such passes, and the related sexual experience, here in Oxford or previously at public school – or both – were accepted features of emotional development. For my Gorbals persona the idea was repellent, but that in itself meant nothing, except, perhaps, that there was something wrong with *me*. Well, I thought perplexedly, if that whole area of experience really was a necessary phase in emotional development, I had no choice but to manage without it.

I reminded myself that I had only Bill's word that it *had* been a pass. Plainly he spoke from experience. His words did seem to fit. Of course, such passes must take many forms. How many times, here in Oxford, had I responded in the 'wrong' manner, misreading the code – *all* the codes? I thought of the many masculine acquaintanceships that had begun in seeming friendly fashion and then, inexplicably, had faded. Was this the reason? Slowly, over the years, I would understand. I had had no conditioning in what continentals sometimes called the English malaise, the sympathetic brotherhood in the boss class which, even if not sexually expressed, was a secure bonding of the spirit, an ineffable guide to 'belonging'. To achieve that special acceptance no brain power, no intellectual curiosity would help me. Like a wrongly scented animal in a herd, I would never belong.

Later in the evening, the crowd having thinned still further and many more bottles emptied, Hannah came up and gripped my wrist. She was deathly pale, not so much frightened as strung taut. 'You must do something! Julian's got a knife. He's hurt someone already!' She pointed to the room beyond the hall, where Bowra had been.

The vibrant hum of party noises was stilled. The expectant silence was almost palpable. Moved by some hypnotic compulsion, I found myself walking across the room with only one thought in mind, a certainty in itself frightening – there was no way out of this. I would confront Julian and get that knife from him – *how* I had no idea. Behind this thought was a troubling question: why was it that not one of these people, now moving aside to let me pass, came to my side to help me? There were so many of them, more than enough – many times over – to overpower one man.

I was the chosen one in a tribal sacrifice, central character in a play of death, all the others frozen in their places in fascination. Why should it be me? What quality, what power, could I possibly have that any one of them did not possess? Perhaps the answer was absurdly prosaic – I was the least drunk. That was too simple, even if it had been true; Werner, for one, diligent host, had so far drunk nothing. Was it that among these people a primitive prudence ruled, which had made them single me out precisely because I was *not* one of them, the brotherhood? What would it matter if *my* blood was shed? Apart from that I was simple enough to be gulled into playing the hero.

All except Bernard. Suddenly he was at my side. I had noticed him refilling his glass steadily, and he swayed a little. He lurched against me. 'Come on, *we'll* sort him out.' He squared his broad shoulders. 'Seen it all before.'

There was a hint of comradely swagger, born of distant bugles: we'll face this together, whatever it is. The poignancy would return, in memory over the years, again and again.

No, I said to myself; he's in no state for a fight, not if Julian's got a knife. I could not, *must* not let him go into that room with me, or there would be disaster. 'No! Stay here.'

'It's all right,' he muttered again, 'done it all before.'

We were at the drawing-room door. Werner stood rooted to the floor like the rest, champagne bottle in one hand, glass in the other – in retrospect a comic, pitiable sight. There was only one solution – I gave Bernard a heave with my shoulder and he toppled over and crumpled at Werner's feet.

Diana, standing near, suddenly clung to Werner, stared at me in terror and said in a strangled voice: 'Oh don't go in there – please!'

I crossed the hall to the open door of the facing room. Julian stood with his back pressed against the far wall, staring fixedly as if possessed; I wondered if he saw me. Round the room, people hugged the wall or cowered behind furniture. A man crouched in a corner, blood dripping from a gash on the back of his hand. As I entered, they edged towards the door and filtered out behind me. Someone whispered as he passed: 'Careful! He's got a commando knife!'

Julian's right hand was by his side, and from it, pointing to the floor, hung the long blade of a heavy knife, broadening towards an angular point. On one of its sloping edges a smear of something red and wet caught the light. He was about fifteen feet away. Cold fear streaked up the back of my neck, but curiously distant as if it was *someone else's* fear. I could not have turned back. I was driven by something already written. The whole world was shut out. Nothing existed but the infernal stare on Julian's face, a mask of sad fury, the dark blue veins bulging out on his neck; and that long blade. Oh God, make him stand still! I must get close, really close. What I would do then, I had only a vague idea.

A thought boomed in my mind like a drum beat. I must project tremendous calm and determination – overwhelm him with my confidence. Confidence? I had none. I felt only that I moved automatically, not with my own will, the slave of some power – God alone knew what or why. A man stood there with murder in his eyes. I must make him understand that I was not bluffing, that I *would* attack; and that he was going to drop that knife. I must go for that wrist. I must not look at the knife lest he be alerted. I tried to remember the army training in unarmed combat, disjointed visions of using the adversary's strength and weight in falls and locks and leverage – to throw, hurt, disable. These thoughts, it occurred to me afterwards, transmitted to him in the electric moments as I steadfastly approached, may have spoken to him more powerfully than words could have done, broken through into his secret world of doubts and demons, dragged him back to reckon with the world as it was.

I would leap for that wrist, trip him off his feet and get a knee on his neck. He was about my height, and quite strong – speed alone must save me. If he continued to stand still there against the wall, all might be well. If he once brought that knife into action, with that terrible blade the length of a small bayonet – God help me.

Slowly, taking short steps, I narrowed the distance, looking fixedly at him, trying to hold his eyes. Now I was ten feet away. He did not move, still stared glassily, but I saw the dark veins bulge on the hand holding the knife. I said, hoping my voice sounded steady, summoning all the menace I could, 'I am going to take that knife from you.' I softened my tone: 'It's better if *you* drop it. Come on, open those fingers and let it fall.' He said nothing. His expression did not change. I moved one more small pace. Another. Another. Five feet away. Now for it! He must have seen my eye flicker to the knife, for the blade rose and the point was levelled at me. I said: 'Drop the knife – *now*.' I tensed to jump. And then – I could not believe it – his fingers opened and the knife thudded to the floor. I leapt forward and kicked it away, facing him, poised for what might still need to be done. The mask of fury had gone. He looked at me in helpless appeal, open-mouthed, gasping with an awesome croaking sound – dreadful reminder of Bernard's father – then his spare form slid down the wall and he fell on his knees, and tears streamed down the lean cheeks; a paroxysm of tubercular coughing seized him, and his lips were wet with bloodstained phlegm.

Cold sweat drenched me. And now it was I who was rooted to the floor, all momentum spent. I stared down into a bottomless abyss of tragedy – beyond the power of all pity, all compassion, all sadness to assuage or cancel. I was sorry to have humbled him, but that was insignificant now. A wave of despair swept over me, not for him alone, for all of us. Gazing down at him, I looked beyond him into the Inferno, into the mind of Dante himself, the world as it really was. In torment, Julian had pulled the mask from himself and from the world too – while the others clung to theirs. That was the only difference between them. He had spoken, in his fashion, for us all.

The others drifted cautiously into the room – wild-eyed, apprehensive. They stared blankly, seemingly with no stir of feeling, at Julian's crumpled figure as he fought to breathe through the barrier of his own blood; they took refuge in the childlike innocence of the tipsy – but not in truth innocent! With their sure instinct for self-preservation they kept their distance in every sense. From behind them came sounds of curses and thumping feet, and Bernard forced his way through the stony ranks, halted and took it all in. He gave me a fierce look – partly in reproof for having excluded him, partly a signal that he was now taking over. This is none of *our* business – yours and mine – but if this lot won't stir a finger to clear up the mess, then *we* must do it!

He could have said that about many things!

His stocky bulk swung round and confronted them, and it seemed that I heard his voice from afar, on some remote barrack square, with the bitter rasp, the full-throated roar of the drill sergeant exercising 'power of command' on a squad of unhappy recruits: 'Come on you lot! Ye've gottae get this poor bugger to a hospital fuckin' quick! Jump to it! – if you don't want the police sticking their noses into everything!' That, he knew well enough, was the last thing any of them wanted. Somebody muttered that the Radcliffe Infirmary was only a-stone's throw away. 'Now you're talking! All right – you, you and you, and you – take his arms and legs, and be fuckin' quick about it!'

Nothing was solid. As when a child shakes the doll's house and sends its contents flying, the world raged about me in fragments, re-fused, came to rest in new juxtaposition – people, perceptions, truths – and now it presented yet another face, cruel, calculating, unyielding. I must begin to comprehend it piece by piece, all over again.

I had stepped into a Breughel painting, and incarnations of people's secret emotions and desires, delicate, savage, insatiable, crowded round me, pulled me this way and that, danced and jeered: 'Do not turn away from what you see! Accept us, acknowledge us, or we will kill you.'

There was shame to be digested, dangerous innocence – or was it deliberate blindness? – unmarked or ignored before.

I went into the deserted drawing room and sat in a corner, in a gilt armchair with back and seat embroidered with silken scenes of Arcadia.

What of the unappetising behaviour of the others? One explanation came to mind, enshrined in a piece of barrack-room wisdom handed down through generations of old sweats: 'Always let someone *else* carry the can for you if anything goes wrong!' That was what they had done to me – these people with their superior boss class airs, their fine public school principles of what was done and what was not.

Perhaps I too should have backed away, as they had done? What then would have happened? Ah no, that was not the question to ask. 'Look after Number One!' the old sweats said: 'That's all you must think about.'

Bernard came in. We sat in silence. After a few minutes he sighed and said, 'How the hell did *you* get lumbered with this? You weren't even *in* that room when it all blew up?'

Much later I would see that there could have been no shortage of catalysts in that *louche* coming together of high and low, of innocence and experience, hard, twisted, predatory, careless in every sense. In many of these people, caught in the mesh of war secrets, the energy needed to keep dangerous knowledge battened down must have clamoured for release in some alternative way, seemingly less dangerous; and for everyone there was the *angst* of the hour. The forces that had exploded in Julian, or rather through him, had been 'par for the course' too.

A few of the remaining guests drifted in. Glasses were refilled. Assurance rose to the surface once again. There was an urge to forget, as when someone has committed a gaffe at a dinner party, and the talk moves on to erase its memory. The trauma, however, persisting beneath the surface, now and then broke through. Hannah, who had observed Bowra stalk out of the drawing-room and into the room opposite, had gathered that he had gone up to Julian, spoken briefly and turned away and briskly left. Another man – the one who had suffered the gashed hand – had then spoken to Julian, who had pushed him violently away. When and why the knife had made its appearance no one knew. The man with the bloody hand had slipped away. Hearing this, Werner sighed with relief.

Bill entered, unperturbed, genial, carrying a bottle of Veuve Cliquot. He handed me a fresh glass: 'Good man! Pity, though. Poor chap's in a bad way. Anyway, the whole thing's best forgotten.'

Bernard held up a glass for a refill. Now that the need for action and control was over, he had resumed the manner of the soldier in his cups.

Draining the glass almost in a gulp, he sucked breath between his teeth and said: 'I've seen a man shot out of hand for pulling a knife like that.'

Diana, her hair in disarray, still clung to Werner as to a lifeline. Perhaps in shock, she said to me, in a troubled, peevish tone: 'You shouldn't have got mixed up in it. Someone else should have . . .' She did not dare continue. 'Anyway, it wasn't your business!'

Werner said stiffly, plainly aware of the undertones, 'I am sorry. I feel responsible, as your host, but what could I do? As a foreigner I have to be so careful.'

Hannah said, 'I couldn't think of anyone else who could cope. Something had to be done quickly.'

Bernard said, carefully, 'It's not a nice thing to say in front of women, but when there are pansies about, some men get nervous about themselves.'

Hannah wrinkled her nose. 'Yes,' she murmured, 'it's true.'

I misjudged Diana, though I did not see it then. In her total detachment, a kind of nihilism, she had been right. None of it was my business; clearing up other people's messes was *their* affair – the people who belonged. I resented what I thought was her refusal to understand – that I had obeyed peremptory forces *within me*, that I had acted for the righteous cause as I saw it, come what may. I was wrong. She did understand. In the confusion of the moment her tumbled words were solely of distress for me, pleading that I should not foolishly go in the way of death. Those who stood back and chose their moment to act in their own interests, let *them* be the heroes of this world!

Yes, her assessment was right; but that in itself was not important. It was I who had been insensitive; I had not *tried* to understand her. Pride overruled sensibility. Stupidly hurt, I was to turn away from her, though at the time it would appear as the inevitable distancing of souls that had ceased to resonate together. Here was yet another piece of self-inflicted pain. I lost *her*, her sensibility, her innocent, uncompromising strength – a wondrous, caring heart.

A few years later, when we were together in London after her marriage to Prince Leowenstein, there would be bitter-sweet sympathy, mutual recognition of loss – too late.

14

Laski: the Still, Small Voice

I wrote to Harold Laski and asked if I might come to see him.

I could no longer postpone an answer to the question: what was to be my next move? Where *could* I go? What should I do? At last I had hit upon an idea. Laski must surely be the right man to talk to about it.

Over and over again my thoughts were drawn back to Alec's words before I left the factory. A recurrent nightmare must have been associated with them. I was trying to walk through a street flooded with some gluey substance, and each time I pulled one foot out to take a step forward the other sank deeper and pulled me back; then some power gripped me and turned me round to face the way I had come, where there was a gigantic creature too terrible to gaze upon, and so I turned away from it and was forcibly turned again, and each time the unseen power gripped me more and more tightly and the swamp held me fast – and I must continue this futile and terrifying struggle for ever. I would wake up shivering in fear.

Across the silences of the years Alec's words brought an acute sense of loss, as yet indefinable. What could I do about it? How? It seemed to be too late. I must follow this road wherever it led, whatever the chagrin and penalty. Did every move in life have a debit side?

Alec had tried to tell me that I was making a tragic mistake in pinning my faith in the things of the mind and letting the heart go unnourished; and that life would take its revenge. In so far as I heard him at all, I had shrugged aside the emotional resonances he delicately tried to convey – not to neglect the vital essences in relationships, awareness, the progress of the soul. I heard the words but not the music – a fault I would repeat again and again:

> 'The words of a song fade on the wind.
> The music speaks to the heart.'

At that time the surface logic of Alec's words had been easy to reject, dizzy with success as I was, seeing nothing but a golden road opening out before me – all other things would surely look after themselves. More profoundly – the music beneath – he had questioned the wisdom of going away at all. The spiritual losses would outweigh the gains. I pretended to myself that I did not hear, but I think I did – at least a hint of it – and shrank away. The thought was intolerable. It would return in increasing strength as the years went by.

From the very beginning I must have assumed that I would never go back to the Gorbals. To do so would be a defeat. Now, as I posted the letter to Professor Laski, I asked myself: would I, given some magical time machine, translate myself back, as if I had never been away, stand again at my old place at the pressing table, resume the old life? Would I, if I could, cancel the Oxford experience altogether? The questions were absurd, but they were an acid test. I touched the callouses on my right hand, plates of hard flesh, once as tough as board and with as little feeling, on the inside pads of the fingers and on the palm – relics of the years I had invested gripping the thick twisted bar of rough metal that formed the handle of the eighteen-pound press iron, and only now beginning to soften and shrink. No. There could be no going back; not to that, not to *anything* in the Gorbals.

There was no weighing of pros and cons. My certainty had little to do with Alec's words, or so I thought. Perhaps, as in the dream, the primordial forces he conjured up were too terrifying to face – spiritual influences I had been too green even to try to understand. Dimly, now, I did begin to understand them. When Alec had spoken of them I had recoiled instinctively; now I did so consciously, with an after-taste of inexplicable bitterness, telling myself that in any case the questions came too late – they were irrelevant now. Time had moved on, the old choices were no longer there. I was changed, and if I did venture back, it would not be in truth a *return*, for I was not the person who had left; and those who remained I would see differently. The old picture – and I myself who had belonged to it – would have disappeared, overlaid as in a palimpsest:

> 'Fare forward, you who think that you are voyaging;
> You are not those who saw the harbour
> Receding, or those who will disembark . . .'

I was not the same person for another reason, in its way just as crucial. In the Gorbals I had believed in absolutes, in black and white – there was one single thread to be found that would guide me through the labyrinth. That sureness was gone for ever. The ideals I had brought away with me may have been wildly unrealistic, but they had given me firm ground, of a kind. Because they had not fitted the new world I had found here, I had let them slip away, never to be recovered; to be replaced by – what? I wished I knew.

What I did know, or rather sensed, was that I *had* moved, profoundly, with hints of new forces at work – as one feels, on a late March morning much like any other, a new tincture in the air, not yet warm but astringent, impatient, the earth quick with new forms as yet unseen, long before the first crocus peeps above the ground. I was shifting to a new course, as yet only a whisper in the mind. I was going to strike out and fashion a new *weltanschauung* of my own – *how* I had no idea – leave behind the received wisdom I had found here, create a new 'cause' to replace the one I had lost. Dimly I saw that I must resume the quest where my scholarship essay had left off – saying 'No' to the question 'Has science increased human happiness?' – and go on to the bitter end wherever that might be. Writing to Laski was the first concrete step.

I had revisited the Gorbals once, and that encounter would last me for ever. Going up to the little flat I was shocked by the filth of the close and the stairs, and the melange of stenches from the flats on each landing, amazed that I had forgotten that this was their proper state. I had felt shame too, as if I stood exposed before my Oxford acquaintances. Why shame, I wondered, I who had flaunted these origins in their faces? Did I think I had risen above the inhabitants of these tenements? Or did I glimpse the shade of my former self here, unquiet spirit haunting the shadows, and fear to meet him face to face – yet powerless to turn my back on him?

Once again, confronting my beginnings, was I daunted by the vision of how far I must travel to escape them – and the thought that I never would?

Father was out at work. The flat looked a little tidier than I remembered it; but every object – the old kitchen table, the lopsided wooden ladderback chairs, the alcove bed beside the stove with its yellowing undersheet and the great 'perraneh' like a huge well-stuffed duvet filled with down feathers, a precious relic of mother's marriage portion brought all the way from *der heim*, flung back against the peeling wall – proclaimed that here was an embattled man living alone; a line was drawn between caring about the essentials of existence and neglecting appearances. The place smelt of damp and decayed food, in a grey twilight even on this summer day, the windows as grimy as I remembered them, the unlit stove still streaked with grease; there were rat droppings in a dark corner. Father's shirt and other washing hung on a string stretched above the long shallow earthenware sink.

He greeted me in somewhat puzzled fashion, stolidly, with perfunctory warmth, wary curiosity. He seemed taken aback by something unfamiliar in my bearing, but especially by my speech: 'Voossfer redstoo azay?' ('Why are you talking like that?'). I did not know what he meant at first. Unconsciously I had dropped the Gorbals twang and now spoke a version of standard English – what the vernacular called 'hoity-toity' speech. I resolved, for the remainder of my stay, to try to revert to the old way of speaking. Alas, it would be as unconvincing here as my acquired diction was in Oxford.

Observing me during long silences, he seemed surprised that I had returned at all. To his way of thinking, once a son had left home he had shaken its dust off his feet for ever. As on that last morning when I had left to ride to Oxford, when we had stood facing one another tongue-tied, he in hat and coat ready to go to work, no words fitted the immense questions that hung in the air between us. He sat across the kitchen table from me, shirt sleeves rolled up, elbows resting on the cracked oilcloth, holding a cup of tea in both hands, the grey-blue eyes looking at me and yet at something far away. They were damp. My new presence filled him with unfathomable perplexities. I felt his love trying to reach me, mysteriously thwarted. He wanted to speak to me, at last, on level terms, to guide me in the next stage of my life – something he had had little stomach for in the past, perhaps because his own guilt intruded. Now, similarly, he must have thought, punishing himself, 'Who am I to tell my son how to run his life, seeing what I have done with mine!' The silences lengthened. Foolishly I tried to fill them with talk of my life in Oxford, and saw an impatience, a sense of despair, cloud the long solemn features, in which I saw, as behind a curtain, a still youthful soul, furtive, anxious, unproven, but in his fashion still undefeated. For him, as always, talk had to be *sub specie aeternitatis* whatever the cost in pain – that or nothing. In any case, these visions I tried to bring him –

hoping to involve him vicariously – came too late. The world I described with the uncertain eagerness of youth was to him not only a foreign land, unknowable, but, more to the point, contained no hint of that better life that was the only reason for a son to leave home. 'Vossgoot kimmt? Vee kanness a bessernlayben verdeenen – mit kayn trade in hant?' ('What good will come of it? How will it earn you a better living – with no trade in your hand?').

He said it from concern, not to hurt. Still, he struck unerringly at doubts of my own.

Lilian and Mary, living in middle-class comfort north of the river, had even less interest in seeing me. I was a reminder of their dereliction; I brought guilt. Stupidly I tried to tell them that the past was forgotten, that we should now think only of the future. Such sentiments, I realised too late, they interpreted as an accusation – to 'forget' the past must mean that it needed to be forgiven. I touched raw nerves. I hurt their pride. Yet to have said nothing about the past would have implied that I too felt guilty about it. That would be unfair; the deeds were *theirs*, not mine, and any guilt must be theirs too. If I offered forgiveness they should accept it with a good heart. Discordant voices spoke out of the unappeased past. With shock I realised that I still looked at my sisters with the eyes of the small child. They were still the great ones moving my small world volcanically. I still addressed them with the humility, the apprehension, proper to long ago, when each word, each fresh sound or gesture, could presage yet another trauma. I still waited for them to put my world together again – knowing they would not. Incongruous, too, was a comic element; here was I, the young brother, a pauper, offering *them* a bounty, a pardon.

When I was older I would see their inflated pride as infantile, and wish that I had been mature enough to regard it with detachment, and refuse to let it sting. And *my* juvenile pride, now asserting itself far beyond its proper time – made the impasse complete.

'. . . it is a stiff-necked people.'

In the years since they had left home, trust and love, the wholesome flow of feeling from a young boy to older sisters – the more crucial because mother had died so young – had bled away. The only common ground lay in the past, and that divided us. So also did subsequent events in their lives, as yet unknown to me, which I would hear about from

---

Mary, in sad confession, after Lilian's death – dark relationships, shifts and compromises, as they strove to 'better themselves'. Conversation was artificial; we searched for safe topics. They expressed surprise that I had sought them out at all; each asked, before many minutes had passed: 'Have you come for money?' – not in the kindly sense of an older, prosperous sister offering a brother a helping hand, but challengingly, as if daring me to say yes. That hurt. The idea of holding out my hand for alms had simply not occurred to me. Certainly, a little extra money would have been of help, and to be fair, had I asked in so many words, I believe they would have given me some; but their tone, perhaps intentionally – knowing me as they did – made certain that I would not ask.

They were frankly sceptical, woundingly so, when I said that I had come, this time enriched by experience, solely to renew contact with my own flesh and blood, hoping for friendship at the very least – to join hands as adults journeying through the world. Perhaps their suspicion came from their guilt – making them as distrustful of me as they knew *they* had earned distrust? They could not believe that I wanted to come near to them for *themselves* alone – there had to be another, suspect, reason.

Their prickly suspicion held a monumental pathos; they were not happy behind their fortifications, and it hurt me to see it. They could not, would not, believe that a warm-hearted word was all I asked, that I sought acceptance as rightfully close to them – a lowering of defences, a sharing of identity.

Instead, there was nothing but a halting exchange of trivia. There were tentative enquiries about father – why wait for *me* to come from afar, in order to ask after him, when he lived no further than the other side of the Clyde? About *my* life they wanted to know nothing – there was no money in what I was doing, either now or in prospect. For them, as for father but for different reasons, I presented too many uncomfortable questions.

The greatest shock came when I met the shower-room group at the swimming baths, people I had met regularly through the adolescent years. At first tongue-tied, aloof, embarrassed, they were finally resentful. Plainly they wished I had not come. Dimly I sensed that my presence, as with father and my sisters, prompted them to look at their lives afresh, and that upset them, the more so because they could not understand why. *They* were certain of what that pattern had to be, and if not content with it they were at least determined to pursue it as they found it – as I had *not*. They hotly rejected such questioning, and blamed their discomfort on me. In retaliation they launched their own barbs at me. They taunted me for my 'proper' speech – 'Whi' are ye talkin' doon tae us for?' They needed to pay me back for having made my escape and even more for returning – as they saw it – to proclaim superiority. I had shown contempt for their life, and for their valuation of themselves. In revenge, they had to reject me.

On the face of it they had some excuse; what they saw could not be denied – though their interpretation was pitifully wrong and no explanation would change it. I *was* no longer one of them. My clothes for instance, sports jacket and shirt and flannels and tie – poor by Oxford standards – were conspicuously middle-class in the Gorbals of shoddy cloth, mufflers and cloth caps. They snarled at me for talking Kelvinside. Above all, I saw different horizons – which they interpreted as being offensively superior. The switch in my life's course was to them enigmatic; indefinably it must be a step up, and envy increased their fury. Yet, to do them justice, deep down at a more mature level, they were suspicious of their *own* stock responses, and their sense of injury mystified them; and so, shaken, tight-lipped, not so much in malice as in frustration, they would talk to me no more. In the streets and closes of the Gorbals I was shunned as a leper.

Unawares, I may have increased their uneasiness, and hence their resentment, by letting signs of my own doubts slip out – insecurity at having broken away from the Gorbals, fear of being sucked back into the old, wounding life. Looking round me in the familiar streets and tenements – familiar but now unknown – I was dismayed to see that even with my new intellectual confidence and sophistication, I could not confront the past calmly – not yet. My old foundations were destroyed and I had still to find new ones to stand on. I had too little faith. I may even have hoped, a greater error still, that the past was finished with, that it would trouble me no more; that I could erase it – even, in fantasy, rewrite it. It would take me many years to look at it with even the beginnings of detachment.

The responses from father and sisters, chilling and sad though they were, were not unexpected – our wounded history had to play itself out to the end. The rebuff from my old friends hit me so hard because, stupidly, I was unprepared. Once again Alec was proved right. I should have expected it; I should have been more *aware*. Perhaps, secretly, childishly, I had dreamed of being greeted as the returning hero. Remembering their cool scepticism at the first news of my scholarship I should have known better. That settled it. I must turn away, now, for ever. I must try my luck where there were no reminders of the past – no spectres of doubt, where that unquiet shade, my *alter ego* from the Gorbals could at last be at peace.

In writing to Laski I was making a start on this new course. My idea was to probe to the heart of an unseen, potentially sinister, Machiavellian factor in government, the little-understood phenomenon of pressure groups, how they worked, influenced opinion, changed attitudes and, above all, political decisions behind the democratic façade; and a newer one, related to it, whose political importance for the future was then unnoticed, the use by caucuses and powerful business interests of the new techniques of attitude measurement or sampling – later to be called, misleadingly, opinion polls – to influence or even 'create' opinion. I wanted to persuade the great man to back the project and let me do the study under his aegis.

To do the work, and write a book on it, I would have to get a research grant, but that would not be difficult with Laski's support.

Laski, third of the socialist heroes I had worshipped from the Gorbals, bestrode, uniquely, the heights of learning and politics. Professor of Political Science in London University, he was in the front rank of the Labour Party leadership and for a time its spiritual and intellectual figurehead.

I was drawn to him for many reasons, most of them indefinable at the time. I think I saw in him a new standard to model myself upon, and in doing so fulfil secret visions of myself. I needed a new figure to occupy the vacant niche where long ago I had placed Einstein. Here was a Jewish firebrand of international distinction as scholar, writer, dealer in the political market place. When he spoke, people listened. What better star to follow?

I had so far seen him only at meetings and lectures, superficially an unimpressive figure, thin, narrow-chested, with a high square forehead under receding dark hair parted in the middle, sallow urchin features with deep lines beside the mouth, thin-framed spectacles with small round lenses, and a narrow moustache which – strange for a Jew to wear at that time – was not unlike Hitler's. In odd contrast with his gruff voice and ramrod bearing was a certain impishness, reflecting his delight in the ideas that bubbled forth in his talk in a coruscating stream. There was assurance verging on arrogance, an American forthrightness then alien to the English milieu, product perhaps of his Harvard years, a bluntness and accent later to be dubbed mid-Atlantic. These attributes, together with his natural bounce and vigour of expression, set him apart from the highly conventional English academics of that time and perhaps repelled some of them. In compensation he had great charm and warmth, the roughness perhaps a surface relic of youthful assertiveness that had out lived its season. When fairly launched into a subject, especially in a formal lecture in his favourite field, French political thought, these disquieting elements faded; and words and cadences flowed elegantly, engaging the imagination like themes in a romantic symphony – something not always present, alas, in his writing, which tended to be involuted and tantalisingly diffuse, defects of his supreme quality, a widely sweeping, impatient mind.

In recent years his star had been in the ascendant – leaving Cole behind – as intellectual leader of the socialist movement as a whole, with Gollancz its brilliant if erratic publicist. In time, however, Laski's highly individual mixture of Continental radicalism, Marxism, and traditional English socialism rooted in Chartism, together with a streak of carefree impracticality, would alarm Labour Party managers as storing up electoral danger in that tense, war-weary time, just as Gollancz's maverick quality was to lead to *his* political eclipse.

The poetic cast of Laski's mind was especially attractive; some of his images would remain with me in all the years ahead. Writing on liberty, arguing that its attainment was an inborn duty, he said that in order to divine its proper use one must 'Listen to the still, small voice within you.' The image was not original. Poe, among others, had used it; and in Laski's usage it expressed the world view of the Philosophes. Still, it was an engaging one, despite its naive assumption that clear sight, and goodwill, resided eternally in the noble savage within us – if we would only set him free. Laski, I suspected, found such imagery irresistible for aesthetic even more than philosophical reasons. Nevertheless, it was sincere, expressing his faith in the perfectibility of Man through reason – which he saw as inseparable from democracy, though how he squared the latter conclusion with his leaning to Marxist *étatisme* was not clear. At all events here he was, nearly halfway through the twentieth century, proclaiming his affinity with the extreme radicalism of the Age of Reason. Not surprisingly the Labour Party of stolid Major Clement Attlee and bluff Ernest Bevin found it hard to live with a Laski who could write thus lyrically of the spirit of the Philosophes: '[together with] faith in the boundless power of reason . . . it is a trust in intuition, a belief that the sentiment within most truly reveals the reality without, which enables us to insist not only upon the natural goodness of man, but also to make the discoveries of reason square with our own desires.'

Such a passage transported me back to crisp Sunday mornings at the speakers' pitch on Glasgow Green, when I stood in ragged shorts and shirt and wet boots looking up at the long lean features of the Clincher, his certificate of sanity rustling in the breeze from the Clyde, bellowing forth his gospel of Burnsian simplicity and innate human goodness; and to saintly Mr Lipchinsky with *his* version of the perfectibility of man; and even to Bernard himself in his days of Marxist dogma. I had come all this way and nothing had changed – except the language.

If the still small voice always guided man's natural goodness correctly, all human affairs would be perfect! When I met him and expressed these doubts, I would find that behind his charm was a juggernaut ready to crush dissent. Like Mr Lipchinsky, he had reached a point in his life where reassessment would feel like sacrilege. I suspect he knew – listening to his own still, small voice – that to talk of the purpose of liberty in this fashion was too facile, almost banal, not addressing the question but avoiding it.

However, this visionary side of him pointed to an engaging sensitivity and innocence, qualities I had assumed would be foreign to a mind so powerful and, as I would discover, so ruthless. Here was yet another romantic held fast in the lofty optimism of the Enlightenment, seeing nothing inconsistent in trying to marry Tom Paine's libertarianism with Marxist state discipline, another dreamer who had outlived his time.

In one short sentence of my letter I had stated the scope of my proposed study, and I was struck by the charm of his replying at once, in his own hand, to invite the unknown student to come for a talk. It would emerge that he had satisfied himself about me by enquiries through the academic network.

At such times of accolade – as when I was 'judged worthy of distinction' – I felt a twinge of regret, of spiritual loneliness, and wished that there had been someone of my own blood, father, sisters, Aunt Rachel or Uncle Salman, who could have shared fulfilment with me.

Making my way from Paddington to his house near Olympia I lost my way, London being unknown territory, and found myself near Broadcasting House instead of much further west. It was the morning after a night of bombing, and as I trudged through streets littered with debris – long shards of plate glass, mangled metal, piled-up broken timber and lumps of stone and brickwork – I saw, towering above an enormous crater filled with the remains of a house, the jagged outline of a shattered party wall which, as I looked, trembled as if it would thunder down at any moment; on it, some thirty feet up, in what must have been a recessed clothes cupboard, a woman's green frilly dress, still on its hanger, swung gently in the breeze. Where was the woman who owned it? Was she under that heap of rubble? I retraced my steps to where I could contemplate again the confident modernism of Broadcasting House, rounded like the superstructure of a great ship, and thought of that early, desperately sanguine motto of radio: 'Nation shall speak peace unto nation'. When would that ever be true? And what was I doing, going to talk to Laski about democracy and the subtle springs and levers of power, in the midst of Armageddon? In a sense Armageddon was with us all the time – all you had were remissions, pauses for breath and hope. All you could do was pretend that each breathing space might endure long enough to see you through your own life.

In a grey Victorian house, the interior scented with furniture polish and the faint acrid aroma of horsehair upholstery, Laski greeted me in a lofty, airy study. He was dressed in a grey suit and, surprisingly, boots. The last time I had seen boots worn with a suit was in the Gorbals; and as he sat down opposite me in a high-backed armchair, legs stretched forward and feet resting on a low stool, the soles of these great boots faced me like huge shields, seeming to loom too large, all but eclipsing him as in a photograph taken at too close range. The shield image, I would discover, was apt.

Early in that first meeting he made an extraordinary Freudian slip. It was evident that he liked to underline his closeness to the Labour leaders in the coalition Cabinet, and one method was to show that he was 'in the know'. Over coffee, before we got down to serious discussion, he gaily remarked *à propos* the night's bombing that 'a few hours ago' a huge bomb had landed close to where Churchill was holding a late-night meeting. Had Churchill been in any danger, I asked? He gave his characteristic rasp of a laugh: 'Not him! *He* was safe and sound in a bunker three storeys above ground!' I said, 'You mean *below* ground?' He looked at me in perplexity: 'What did I say?' I told him. He frowned, out of countenance, then laughed again: 'Good gracious, of course I don't wish him out of the way – *not yet!*'

The little moustache lifted as he smiled in complicity; then he changed the subject.

He began to talk about my proposed study, especially the political implications. I had a twinge of foreboding. It would, he said, attack the workings of government, and of parties, probably quite damagingly? I said that was precisely what I hoped to do. As if on cue, he launched into a series of leading questions, a Socratic dialogue: 'Do you not agree that . . .' and 'If so, then . . . ?' He was trying to drive me into a corner, but what corner? In my innocence I thought he was simply testing my conviction, and my competence to carry out the study. Thinking only of defending my idea, and shining in this elegant disputation, it did not occur to me that he might be trying to talk me out of doing the study altogether. I told myself that he *must* be interested in my ideas about it, otherwise, surely, why would he bother to arrange this meeting? After about an hour he looked at his watch. 'I'm giving a lecture at the Senate House at twelve. Come along, we can talk in the taxi.' The lecture would be on French political thought after the Revolution. We would need to meet again, he said. We fixed another day for me to visit him.

The taxi – this was to be my very first experience of one – must have been already booked, for in a few minutes a bell sounded far away in the bowels of the house. On the outer step, the cabbie touched his cap to the great man, greeted him with the friendly formality of an old retainer – 'Morning, professor' – and with some ceremony led the way down the few yards of path to hold the cab door open. The vehicle had an old-fashioned cabriolet body, the driver's compartment open – apart from windscreen and roof – where he sat, as in horse-drawn days, with a piece of black tarpaulin over his knees against the weather.

As we bumped along on the old springs, Laski said, thoughtfully, 'It is a mistake to think we've got democracy in this country. In theory we have but it's really an electoral oligarchy! We need to widen the true franchise – but that's for the distant future.' By 'we' he meant the socialist movement, in particular the Labour Party as its 'conformist' vanguard. All the same, he added, we shall have to use the system *as it is*, with all its falsifications – the things *you* are worried about for example, your pressure groups and opinion sampling, all the tricks of opinion management. In fact they might actually help us to get our hands on power. Power first – improvement afterwards!

Where had I heard that before, or something very much like it? Yes, from Bernard when he came back from Spain, having abandoned the dogma of 'abolish or nothing' and instead determined to make do, to use the system as it stood.

Laski's words should have warned me. Despite his earlier show of scepticism, in that moment of frankness he revealed that he saw the future very much as I did but without alarm, indeed with something like virtuoso glee – the death of the hustings, the supremacy of marketing techniques in political life, unashamedly selective, finely tuned to 'consumer profiles'. He not only recognised the 'falsifications' of democracy that I wanted to correct, but was content to leave them untouched. Sensing imminent electoral victory for Labour, he saw himself making use of them soon, and doing so ruthlessly. The parallel with Kerensky occurred to me, far from exact but near enough; he dreamed of himself as that impossible hybrid, a Leninist Kerensky.

He may have realised the slip, for he veered away. 'We need,' he said, 'to get closer to the working class! Some of my good students go to work in the East End to get to understand the workers. You too, I should say, need to learn how the workers tick! I could help you get some social work in the East End if you like.'

I had forgotten to tell him that I came from the Gorbals. That showed how far I had travelled. Here was a strange reversal. Long ago it was I who had told Crossman that *he* should learn something about the workers; and now – how could it be? – here was Laski telling *me* to do so! Luckily, at that moment, the taxi passed through the tall gates of the Senate House and swung to a halt in the forecourt; otherwise I might have told him about the Gorbals – and too bluntly. When, at our next meeting, I did tell him, he would remember his words and grin in salute. Quizzically, drawing in the thin lips under the symbolic moustache, he would say, echoing Bernard, 'You *have* done a good job on yourself – no one would have thought it!' And I would wonder if there was a hint of the envy I had seen on Crossman's face.

In the main entrance hall, Cyclopean, stark, mechanistic – reminding me of the approach to the machine hall in Fritz Lang's futuristic film *Metropolis* – his foot on the bottom step of the great staircase leading to the Macmillan Hall where he was to lecture, he abruptly turned: 'Say, d'you know where I can have a cock here?' It took me a couple of seconds to decode the question; he wanted to go to the lavatory. Why ask *me*? Here he was on his own territory; he knew I had never set foot in the place before. However, I owed the great man respect; I turned towards the long reception desk nearby, intending to ask one of the uniformed staff. He stopped me, saying gruffly 'The hell with it, I'll manage without,' and with springy step led the way upstairs. Once in the Hall, he courteously led me to a seat in the front row, mounted the dais, and without any notes, delivered an entrancing, evocative, exquisitely phrased discourse, full of gentle poetry. There was not a sign of the Leninist Kerensky.

Bernard said, 'You are barking up the wrong tree with Laski. *He* won't help you with this pressure group idea of yours. It's obvious. He doesn't want to be seen to be spreading doubts about the machine, especially *now* – with the Labour Party girding up its loins for a victory election, and to become, at last, a governmental party. He's just stringing you along! He can see you're full of ideas, perhaps like *he* was when he was young, and he wants to keep you hanging around so that he can pick your brains when he wants to. That's the way a "has been" thinks!'

Once again we chewed over the future. The switch from revolutionary soldier to toiler in the trade union vineyard had been good for his soul as far as it went; but now he dreamed again of shifting the world, this time through legitimate radicalism, in Parliament. Sniffing the wind, he predicted a Labour victory. Now a national figure in the union, close to Labour Party inner circles, he had been offered a constituency. Why didn't I take that road too? A swift 'demob election' was on the cards. The party managers, privately, were not speaking of victory, but at the

very least aimed to fill the opposition benches with new talent. 'You're
the kind of material they're looking for! Constituencies are going begging.
I could put a word in for you. As things are, I think you'd get one.'

He would bet money on us both getting in. Time, however, was critical.
There was going to be a governmental scheme for service people overseas
seeking adoption as parliamentary candidates to be flown back to this
country to face constituency selection committees. Now, therefore, before
that flood began, was the moment to act.

He echoed Laski's reckoning. Old loyalties were giving way to new
calculation. It would not be *principle* that would turn the country upside
down, but an automatic revulsion against an old élite drained of the
confidence of fifty years before, and now seen as inept, dull-witted,
palsied – typified by the spectre of Neville Chamberlain.

Bernard was tougher now than he had ever been. He had acquired a
manipulative streak I would never possess. That old, steady look of
his, the eyes gleaming like dark cherries, had become contemplative,
magisterial, charismatic; he could wait, temporise, scheme, calmly contrive compromises as stepping stones to the ideal. I knew I could not
equal these attributes – not yet, if ever. The route he suggested demanded
a pragmatism, an opportunism, a pretence of certainty as a means of
manipulating people, which I could not stomach. Not yet. I must find
myself first. *He* did not need to; in essence he was what he had always
been. His trials and dangers and heartaches had tempered him, the basic
substance was unchanged. For that I had always admired him, and envied
him. I had no such solidity: all within me seemed freshly minted, with
no history, as if I were my own new creation – as in some ways I was.
Each new step demanded new questioning, new assurance to be bred
within. I was certain of one thing only; I would try to create a new world
through writing. How, in what form, I did not know as yet; I knew only
that I would continue the quest begun long ago in the scholarship essay.
For as far into the future as I could see, that would be my pilgrimage.

As for Laski, it was hard to accept Bernard's verdict. However, he had
had many opportunities to assess Laski, and far more experience of the
world; and I respected his judgment. I must wait and see.

I could not wait for long. Now, more than ever, I felt the burden of
travelling alone. Foolishly, I had sometimes tried to explain this thought
to people here; you felt stronger if you knew that a home hearth existed

somewhere, even if you visited it only in spirit; its *existence* was the crucial thing – a fixed point of support awaiting you always, for you to conjure up in the imagination at moments of doubt, and draw comfort from the knowledge. Without it you were always vulnerable, like a commander with no reserves to fall back on. They listened politely, resisting insight; most of them affected to despise family links: 'You're jolly lucky not to have a family to tie you down!' In truth they were deeply dependent, evidenced by their unease at the subject being broached at all – yet another topic it was not done to talk about. It was too near the heart.

Ken Tynan would sum this up, and the Oxford experience too, with characteristic incisiveness and astuteness, quite early in his time here, in his days of stick-like thinness, the purple suit flapping on him as on a skeleton, his sunken cheeks and lips stretched tight over jutting teeth reminding me, incongruously, of the Clincher's cadaverous features: 'There's nothing to be got from this place of any value, except maybe a few contacts. Oxford's only use is to give you a stage to strut on and promote yourself! And that's what I'm good at!'

Tynan understood himself well. Happily, shrewdly, he used money and contacts to promote himself; and would have been amazed, like everyone else, were the strategy thought worthy of curiosity or comment. This too, as Bill would have said, was 'par for the course'.

Sometimes the grapes were sour.

Certainly I envied them their home base and ready-made network of people who could open doors; and berated myself for doing so. Envy was poisonous, I told myself – and anyway changed nothing, except to lower the spirit. But it was hard to be free of it; and perhaps that was why, trying to avoid the poison, I seemed to make friends more easily with other *déraciné* people like Werner and Domenico. If true, it was only part of the reason; sharing isolation was in itself a source of warmth – of a kind.

Tynan was not all display and calculation. Hidden away in his unique mixture of banality, tinsel brilliance and showmanship, was a mysterious, startling insight, revealing itself in the telling comment, apt as an arresting newspaper caption but containing much more – at its best a profound personal concern, shyly displayed and then hidden once again beneath the raucous and the superficial. At a sherry party, *à propos* of nothing, he said to me: 'Trouble with you is that you're after the old master stakes and nothing else will do. I'm too impatient for that.'

———

He said it with a mixture of wonder and sadness, almost of commiseration, ostensibly for me – but it might have been for himself too? I could not be sure.

If Laski did fail me, I would find a desk job – not too demanding – and write. It so happened that I had been offered a job at the British Council, part of which was then accommodated in Oriel. That would be a curious alignment – a Gorbals boy purveying British culture! Why not? I could probably do it as well as anyone else, probably better than someone like John Betjeman, with his aristocratic acerbities and addiction to undergraduate satire of the British way of life.

Another irony had struck, momentous and terrible, that I would never understand, whose tragic overtones – sounding far back in time – I would never wholly digest. Father had given up gambling!

He had come to the decision – how I would never know, for he stubbornly refused to discuss it – shortly after my first, disappointing, return visit to the Gorbals. If only he had done it all those years ago when mother was alive! It was as if, with my going away again – this time, he was sure, never again to own the place as home – the last relic of his past life, wounded and wounding, had gone too, and nothing remained for his gambling to destroy.

As a result, he saved money in the Post Office, lived comfortably, probably more so than he could remember, apart from those brief spells when he had been flush after a win at the Faro table. At last he had forsaken the scene of mother's death, and discarded the mattress, on trestles in the kitchen alcove, on which she had died. He had moved to a small flat in the slightly more respectable quarter of the Gorbals near the Talmud Torah in Turriff Street, where he had a bedroom separate from the kitchen, a bathroom and separate lavatory. There, in his practical fashion, he looked after himself well, read a great deal, played solo whist in the Workers' Circle, spent hours chewing over the world with friends. He had several suits, smoked Balkan Sobranie cigarettes in a long amber holder with a gold band. Still, it could not be a happy finale to *his* pilgrimage. Guilt certainly persisted. His world, his life, he tacitly acknowledged, was past rearrangement. No further battle was worth fighting; but at last he was *free*. It was a Pyrrhic victory thus to be left, at the end, alone on the field. The freedom he had won must have been sour in the mouth.

As for my life, he had ceased trying to understand what I was doing with it. He thought me foolish to have challenged this new world single-handed. Having made that clear, he would not speak of it again. In effect he said, trying not to be too harsh, make your own mistakes, as I made mine, and take the consequences.

Separated in our widely different orbits, by some magical shift we had become comrades, on better terms than we had ever been. Here was yet another change that had come about at the wrong time, too late to be of serious use – or comfort – to either of us. Perhaps nothing ever happened at the 'right' time – whatever that was? No! Surely nothing could ever be totally too late? Yes. Some things were.

The fires of the past burned fiercely still. Accusations, claims and counter-claims, gyrated like demons of the Inferno, unappeased. None could be spoken of out loud. Yet there were questions I longed to ask. How long had he known that mother had cancer? Even allowing that he did not know, in those obscurantist days, that it was cancer, he must have had *some* idea that she was seriously ill. Why could he not steel himself to give up gambling then, knowing that the grief and hardship it brought must hasten her end? As for Lilian and Mary, would they have chosen to flee for safety if, seeing the rifts growing, he had stifled his pride and tried to heal them?

The enigmas were poisonously interwoven. It was surely too late to confront them? If only I could hear *his* reasoned account, his verdict. Sometimes, vicariously, I felt his guilt festering within *me*. Perhaps I carried with me, unrecognised, a memory of fearful efforts as a child, seeing him suffer, to share his inscrutable burden. Alas, to press him for answers would now be cruel, and futile – and in any case the truth would come too late. Or could truth ever come too late?

I could not bring myself to do it.

One day, facing each other at his kitchen table, covered with new oil-cloth in a fresh red check pattern, drinking 'Russian tea' – black tea in a glass, sucked through a lump of sugar – he said, 'Remember that fight in the umbrella shop – you were only a little boy then?'

Oh yes I remembered all right – and even now could shudder at the immediacy of that volcanic, ferocious scene – my little world fallen in fragments, father covered in blood, the shop furniture and stock shattered as the three brothers clashed in fury – two united against him.

'Yes,' he said, 'I see you do. I want you to promise me something. If you ever run into them or anyone connected with them, "Zogg azay: mit letsten ottom finsterniss woonshich" ("Tell them this: with my last breath I will curse them with darkness").'

He said it quite calmly, the grey blue eyes solemn, clear, unflinching.

In the context, the dreadful statement included Lilian and Mary.

What could I say? Our new-found comradeship was fragile. Certain topics remained, in sunken menace like an old minefield, too dangerous to approach. In him there could be no forgiveness. Within the family, blood must always be thicker than water; that was paramount. However badly you behaved, punishment must not hit you too cruelly. No sin or omission of his could have merited what his brothers had done to him – above all throwing him out of the partnership in the shop – and what Lilian and Mary had done. He was saying, in effect, '*If* I had done anything wrong, what they did went too far!' This was the nearest he could come to accepting responsibility for *part* – part only – of all that had happened. What had mother done to *him*, I wondered, to merit the retribution of his gambling?

It was all too late.

All right, father, I will tell them.

I never did meet the uncles. As for Lilian and Mary, I did not tell them. But I owe it to him, even this late in the day, to set down these words of his without judgment. They have to be proclaimed as he wanted them to be; and, I still believe, as he deserved them to be – right or wrong! – a last trumpet blast of defiance. To me, inevitably, he must remain a hero, solitary, for all I know totally misunderstood, who communed honestly with his own transcendental voices, who fought the Chimera fearlessly and stubbornly – and lost. Or did he really lose?

That trumpet blast would continue to ring out down the years.

Guilt at having left father on his own returned often. I told myself that there had been no other way. It was not true; there *had* been. There always was. Could I have chosen to stay? Lilian and Mary had had that choice too; their decision to go, bitter for me as a little boy, must have hit father unimaginably harder. He had never, by the slightest hint, reproached me for going, as he had blamed *them*. Not explicitly, but in his own quiet way, he made it plain that I must not take their guilt on to my shoulders. My case was quite different. In his eyes I had done what any young man of spirit could be expected to do – what he himself had done. And though pride would never permit him to say that he was lonely, his expression said – with an imaginary shrug of stoic acceptance – 'Es shtayt geshreeben'.

Lilian and Mary prospered. Their coolness continued. What harm had I done them? None that I could think of. Perhaps, in leaving father, I had underlined *their* desertion, for the tradition said that daughters did not leave home to seek their fortune. Paradoxically, even my failure to ask for their help gnawed at them. My buoyant independence, even in poverty, they could explain only by madness. Or something even more frightening, unworldliness, for that questioned the values they clung to, the fulfilment for which they had cheerfully sacrificed me. Imprisoned within their fortifications, they remained troubled. That, in part, was *their* punishment.

Lilian had become a pillar of charitable effort in Glasgow. Was that her way of expressing remorse – intercession for the soul before the Seat of Judgment? Or was it simply one more manoeuvre in the interests of business?

Their detachment hurt. I tried to see my behaviour from their point of view. Did they feel they must keep my unworldliness at arm's length, lest by association it damaged their standing among the worldly? That was not wholly their fault. They were victims of their milieu. One day, Lilian having asked me to visit her at her office – she would 'fit me in for a few minutes' – I arrived just as she was showing out a client, a gross, middle-aged version of the assertive Phil Emet who had got Annie into trouble. With scarcely concealed unwillingness she introduced us – he was in the *shmattah* business, the rag trade. Her feelings must have transmitted themselves to him, for with an aggressive leer he said: 'An Oxford student, eh! I'm proud of you – but d'you know what's worrying *me*? I've got money coming out of my ears, now what d'you say to that?' He was putting me down with a vengeance, according to his lights. Why, I wondered, did people like him feel so defensive?

Stung, I answered him: 'Am I supposed to feel sorry for you?' He was startled, and the anger burst out: '*You* – feel sorry for *me*!'

'*You* said you were worried – I didn't!'

He was shorter than me, and overweight, but looked quite strong; for an instant, seeing the blood rush to his face, it looked as if he might lash out at me. I thought of the time, all those years ago in the school playground, when I got a beating for challenging another little boy for calling me a 'sheeny' – and here I was facing a like hatred – again for the crime of being different from the herd; this time from a Jew. Nothing had changed.

When he had gone, Lilian said, pale with fury, eyes red and damp behind the thick round lenses, 'That was an important client. He didn't mean any harm. I will have to grovel to excuse your behaviour. You had better not come here again.'

Mary moved to London. Years later, when I too was living there, she would ring me up one day: 'I've just realised, thinking about what the Nazis did to the Jews – that some of *our* relatives over there must have been among them! I didn't think of it before. Do you want to come over and talk about it? I can offer you some good Scotch.'

I should not have replied in the way I did, but this innocence so late in the day – about terrible things now common knowledge – carried another, intolerable implication, that she chose to be equally innocent about the events of our own past. Bitterness overflowed. Before I knew it the words were out: 'There are a lot of things you didn't think about at the right time.'

I was ashamed. After all, she was holding out a hand to me; and I was being self-righteous, in some ways like father, sticking implacably to principle. Yet I longed for true feeling; no superficial substitute would do. Instead she was trying, in her fashion, to put a lid on the past with weak sentiment, or rather to pretend that neither of us remembered what had happened. What would it have cost her, or Lilian, after all this time, at least to acknowledge the possibility – as father had done for his own deeds – that their leaving home might have caused me suffering, and express remorse? 'I felt I had to. I didn't *realise* what it would mean to you' – as perhaps they hadn't! That would have been *something*. But no; she too could not bring herself to utter it – not a single word of doubt or regret.

15

Winners and Losers

Bernard was right about Laski. To be fair, Laski's opposition to my idea was a proof of his clear-sightedness. He was not being obscurantist, simply Machiavellian. Implicitly he admitted that he shared my view of the forces I wanted to expose and how they were likely to change society. But that was bleak comfort.

He stonewalled beautifully – full of charm and sparkle and warmth. Almost in the same breath he maintained that the work I wanted to do was not necessary 'at the present time', and that in any case it had all been done before. Superficially the first statement contradicted the second – though of course 'not necessary' was code for politically inconvenient. The second statement could not possibly have been true. The pioneer work of Mass Observation, for example, though it contained clear and dramatic pointers to the future, was only two years old when it was suspended for the duration of the war. True, the psychological and statistical principles were known – at least to specialists – on which would be based the massive post-war expansion, into almost every corner of life, of attitude measurement, opinion sampling, 'consumer profiling' for product design and sales promotion, including the selling of politicians and programmes; but their probable uses and consequences, especially their social impact, had still to be examined and understood.

He would not admit to political reasons for opposing my project, but the signals for me to drop it were plain. I pretended not to see them. What possible harm could my work do?

'Harm?' He repeated the word with a touch of pique. The round spectacles glinted as he shook his head. 'None at all. You wouldn't dig up anything we don't know already. As for what you say about "bending" opinion – creating bias – what's wrong with that? What politician in his right mind wants to cut out *bias* among the electorate – that is, bias in his favour! Bias in itself is not unfair! An "unfair" bias is one that doesn't suit your book that's all. What do you expect from the electors – the pure

light of reason! Come off it. We are working in a good radical cause –
and if we can bend the bias in our favour, so what? It's a tough old world
my boy, and you'd better get used to it.'

I murmured: 'The end justifies the means – do we ever escape from
that?'

He leaned back with a chuckle, crossed the great boots, and gave a sly
smile at the ceiling as if to say 'What do you want? It's the way of the
world.' Then he resumed the mien of the serious savant: 'Now look here.
I'm going to give you some good advice. There is a lot in what you say
– if there weren't, I wouldn't still be talking with you! Bright young men
love to tilt at received opinion – we've all done it in our time. But don't
go too far or you'll make an awful lot of enemies. In the real world – and
politics is part of it whether you like it or not, though I often wonder
about it myself – it's called rocking the boat. And that makes a lot of folk
uncomfortable and they don't like it, believe me. They could make life
hard for you.'

In itself, it was good advice, but it was hard to conceal bitterness. He
was simply protecting his own position, as he saw it, or rather political
life in general, for him and for others. In fact, had he given me his
support, it would probably have made no difference to *his* political future;
but neither of us could know it. His political importance was about to
end. Naive as I was, I expected honest opposition – instead of sheltering,
as he did, behind specious objections.

That phrase, rocking the boat, was to haunt me in all the years ahead
– in business and institutional affairs, in international life; it encapsulated
the most wounding lesson I would learn since leaving the Gorbals, that
the questioning mind is seldom welcome anywhere. Was mine less
welcome than most? Was I too impatient, or did I blunder because, as
Bill had hinted, I did not 'know the ropes' – how to manoeuvre and
persuade by guile and finesse? There would always be some people to
be upset, guarding special interests, inertia, or simply the desire for a
quiet life – and some would strike back with feline stealth and ferocity.
Many years later, when I was in Budapest as vice-chairman of an
international congress, a charming Rumanian official representative –
doubtless anxious to avoid suspicion of being influenced by my Western
views – would express this disquiet to me with outstanding frankness:
'Monsieur, je suis *ineducable*!'

I admired his honesty.

Laski remained friendliness itself. 'I enjoy talking with you. Please come whenever you want. My door will always be open to you – and I will help you, as I said, if you want to do some social work.'

Social work stank of condescension, or wrong-headedness in diverse guises, pompous, opportunist, fey, self-deluding. I thought of the Glasgow do-gooders with their 'fresh air fortnights' for tenement children as a cure for deprivation. The voyeur, the troubled mind, seemed drawn magnetically to the lower depths where, under various concealments, it sought balm for inner conflicts – like Maugham's missionary in *Rain*, concealing shackled lusts with good works among the heathen – or solace for upper-class guilt, or freedom to experiment in safety with other people's lives. This was still the epoch of smart primitivism among some of the upper-class *avant garde*. Affecting to see the poor as the salt of the earth, they could not get close enough to them – that is, safely so! It was partly a self-indulgent conceit, partly a sincere, if confused, rebellion against suspect values.

Perhaps some upper-class people condescended with a clear conscience, a version of *noblesse oblige*? How could a Gorbals boy presume to counterfeit that?

If I had had time – that is money – Laski's refusal would not have been a blow. I could have dispensed with backers and, like other people here, gone ahead with the work at my own expense. I thought of Rachel – if only! – and guilt washed over me. How could I think of her in this selfish way? I thought of her often, but not for this reason. Yes, I had to admit it, the thought was there: *if* I had sunk my pride and gone to live with her and accepted her money, she would be living still, and there would have been no shortage of funding now. I could have followed any path I pleased, and not been forced, as I was now, to abandon the project and get the first serious job I could – one more 'might have been' of life.

As to Rachel, Bernard had probably been right in that too – if I had really wanted her, as he had remarked, I would not have been afraid to accept her money. That was a bitter thought. How true was love if pride could thwart it?

Looking round, there were reasons in plenty to count one's blessings. Richard, a partially-sighted student, had come to Oxford from a school for the blind, and was reading law. I got to know him through a friend of his, Vincent, also virtually blind and from that school, who lived in the same house as I did for a term; I often helped them with set questions by reading a 'crib' to them. By chance I also knew Richard through his sister Betty. Richard was tall and sturdy, ruddy-faced, with a shock of reddish hair; he had a keen and sensitive mind, and much natural charm. With a prodigious memory, and a feel for the law, a good career awaited him, he said, as a solicitor. I could not know what 'partial sight' meant, but from hints they unintentionally gave, and the way they moved about a room and handled objects, feeling their surfaces and outlines to understand them, I got the impression that all they saw was a greyish blur of light and dark. I was amazed, and sometimes alarmed, by the way these two men lived their lives with dash and confidence; it was wrong, I knew, to admire them for seemingly making light of their disability, for what else could they do? After dinner Vincent would light up a cigarette, operating the lighter near his nose to feel the heat of the flame; he always knew, presumably by a change in the feel or temperature of the cigarette, when it was time to reach for the ash-tray and knock the ash off. Walking in the street, I marvelled that they guided their progress by the echoes of their footsteps – their shoes steel-tipped on heel and toe – sensing gaps in pavements and between houses, even the width of a crossing and the proximity of vehicles and people. They did everything with an ease of usage, an expansive reaching out to the world – seemingly not hermetically locked in inner darkness as the sighted person supposed; but who could tell? They did their best! And I would say to myself: 'Dear God, who am I to think that I am disadvantaged?'

Betty had rosebud lips, gentle brown eyes and a wonderful glow in her cheeks – innocent, tender, with not a trace of the flippant arrogance of the smart set. Our close friendship was platonic; it could have gone beyond that, and perhaps it should have done. We swam in the river beside the great sweep of Port Meadow. When the river path was deserted, seeing the spires and domes of the city far in the distance, beyond fields and marching willows and sentinel poplars, we could imagine ourselves in one of those romantic paintings of northern Italy showing rural simplicity in the foreground and the enigmatic city on the horizon, an Arcadian interregnum of our very own. Afterwards we lay on our backs in the grass under the walls of ruined Godstow Abbey and watched the clouds slide past in the wide sky, talked and were silent, and talked without words through our silences.

After the turbulence and tragedy of Rachel, the egocentricities of Diana, Hannah's unpredictable switches between Amazonian assurance and fragile dependence, I may have been drawn to Betty as a peaceful contrast – but even if true as a motive, that thought took nothing from the bright gleam of her spirit, her grace, her dancing heart.

Once, staying on in Oxford after Betty had gone home, I did not see her for a few weeks. On her return I sensed a sinister stillness in her, as if part of her normally vibrant self was frozen, closed-off and silent. After a while I asked 'How is Richard?' She went pale. Gently she said: 'So you didn't hear?' Richard had gone up to London and fallen under a Tube train as it came into a station and been killed. Our tears mingled, and we were silent for a very long time.

Richard had been anxious about his approaching Schools. Betty said he had no need to be; his tutors had been confident that he would do well.

On a dark evening a year or so later, Betty stepped off the pavement to cross St Giles; the exact sequence of events I never discovered, but according to one account, as she threaded her way among parked cars filling the ill-lit space between the pavement and the line of trees fringing the wide thoroughfare, a car suddenly reversed towards her and she, trying to avoid it on a cobbled patch slippery from recent rain, must have missed her footing and was thrown against another car, hitting her head on it. She was taken to hospital in a coma, and remained enclosed in it, beyond reach, for many months. She never awoke.

The circumstances seemed so bizarre, so improbable, that I looked beyond them and wondered what force had been at work, what fate, which she, half-aware, welcomed?

After going down she had taken a job in Oxford, so that she could stay on and be near Richard, feeling her responsibility as an older sister. In the past year she had let slip a sense that she had failed him.

Had I failed *her*, given too little, *demanded* too little, shared less than I should have done? How many moments had there been in her heart, poised between joy and emptiness, when she had hoped for a step closer from me, in commitment, in revelation – and that vital movement had not come?

———

For many days I moved automatically, senses numbed. I too could willingly have stretched out a hand to welcome the darkness. Recovering, it seemed that mourning too – or rather misery – could hide self-indulgence. Who had the right to judge, theorise, be detached – preempt the Fates? Had father done so, contemplating mother's death? No – that thought too was forbidden. And yet, pacing my room at night, fists clenched, fingernails sometimes drawing blood in the palm, I told myself again and again that things could have been so different – if only! If only I had returned her love without restraint, fortified her with sensitivity – and myself too.

When would I cease to wait for certainty, delay movement till the turning world compelled me, so often too late? How many years, how many lives, dared one let slip:

> '. . . what a dusty answer gets the soul
> When hot for certainty in this our life?'

For what it was worth I was not the solitary loser, but one among a multitude. Annie, Rachel, Diana, Betty, Bill, Bernard, Werner . . . the list stretched out to the horizon. All – each in their own way – belonged to the company of losers.

Where were the gilded winners I had seen on every side in my first days here?

16

Whispers in the Enchanted Forest

Only now, on my first morning on the staff of the British Council, seated in my office in Oriel looking out through leaded panes on a quiet grey stone inner quad, did my transition from the factory seem at last complete. The room had a huge desk – at least it seemed so to me, about six feet long – with two telephones on it, a side-table, bookshelves, several chairs. And I was actually being paid to sit here at my ease, to read letters from romantic-sounding outposts abroad – from cultural attachés, Council representatives – organise supplies, and dictate replies. How could this compare with heaving that eighteen-pound press iron in the steam and clatter and sweat of the factory, the hectic pace of piece work, the corrosive fatigue? Here was civilisation, clean hands, a sense of a place in the world!

I looked back on the years between with a sense of unreality, ineffable, fugitive – whispers in an enchanted forest. Despite the early shocks – the timid arrival at the citadel gates from the lower depths, self-doubt, the brief stage of being patronised as a freak – the first period here had had the feeling of being at a continuous, magical party. I had floated in miraculous freedom through a gilded world, a wondrous minuet of rank and privilege beyond anything I had imagined in the Gorbals, discovery and self-discovery, glory in ease of achievement, the days sparkling and short, too short. The second period, after the army, had been magical in a different style: a *revenant*, partly worldly-wise, partly disillusioned, I was at last beginning to select experience instead of submitting to it blindly, to observe with detachment this turbulent wartime city, aware of apocalyptic change, the Fates stirring the crucible in the sky, myself hurled about within it.

That day of reassessment, when I stood at the corner of the High and the Turl and tried to see where I was and where I should go, *could* go, seemed another age. Certainly I had not got from Oxford what I had come for. For one thing, my romantic vision of it – from the Gorbals –

as the home of the pure, gentle savant, tolerant, worshipping wisdom and sweetness and light whatever the cost, had been ridiculously false. Behind the shallow refinement it could be as ferocious as the Gorbals, in some ways more so, for the Gorbals did not pretend to be other than what it was! And where had Oxford's old, slow, confident pace been heading? That perspective was fading in the sunset mists of Empire, effortless superiority, the *hubris* of 'Gentlemen v. Players'. Yet who was I to criticise it? Was it sour grapes again, seeing that I had arrived too late to join the Gentlemen, their day already fading? Still, they *had* been certain of where they were going, and surely confidence was all that mattered? I thought again of the red sandstone crenellated railway bridge sprawling wide-legged over the Clyde, a declamatory voice of Victorian certainty dominating the speakers' pitch at Glasgow Green where Bernard and the Clincher had once proclaimed their contrasting hopes for man. That assured voice had been heard here too. Stupidly, I had hoped to be infected by that certainty. With it I would surely know *where* to go? I had failed to hear the hollow note within it. Now, even the pretence had gone. The confident pace, the Galsworthian 'sniffing' at other standards, had withdrawn into the shadows, to wither in North Oxford.

The dream of finding a philospher's stone to cure man's ills had been childish – though old Mr Lipchinsky had believed it. Certainly the torch he had passed on to me was now extinguished, and with it the foolish fancy that I would unlock all doors, all secrets, all relationships, life itself, simply by being brainy. In any case, which doors did I now want to open? I was not sure. Still, I had proved myself intellectually, but I had paid for it; I had scaled magic heights and found obscurantism, absence of hope, a world infinitely darker than I had ever imagined possible from where I had stood in the Gorbals. Yet here I was, with the British Council, committed to project the complacent boss class view – the word 'establishment' was not yet current – of where we all stood. Aside from Lord Beaverbrook's obsessional jibes about the Council's élitism, its lack of realism in sending Morris dancers and Elizabethan lute players to portray Britain in foreign lands, one could fairly say that the Council projected the British way of life as seen from the top, seemingly unaffected by the surge of history – the sunset of Imperial Britain was as yet only whispered. That the Council worked under the aegis of the Foreign Office gave credence to this view. To do my job at the Council, even in my junior position, I felt I must believe in the establishment view – if not believe, then at least be at peace with it. Amazingly, I found that easier than I had feared.

Was it mere opportunism? After all, the Council was giving me a living! Or had I lost my bearings altogether? I was learning a simple, obvious truth – not obvious then – that nothing in life was all bad. Many progressives in the Council, shocked by the horrors of Nazism and Fascism, found grim consolation in the thought that the British way of life, even though unfortunately capitalist, was not so bad after all. Others, more or less apolitical, such as John Betjeman and Louis MacNeice, would sometimes appear uneasy at certain aspects of it. This ambivalence was neatly expressed when a colleague at the Council, later to achieve distinction as a poet, sent me a copy of his first slim volume of verse with a note: 'This is to get you into trouble with the secret police!' A characteristic irony, for the poems were far from subversive; the reference, I think, was rather to what he *could* have written but had suppressed. In the general feeling of shifting sands, the sentiment was understandable.

The knowledge that I was not alone in my insecurity was not comforting – if anything it was disturbing, for everyone else seemed to deal with it more competently. They retreated from innocence into a wary, opportunist view of life, concealed beneath an urbane rapprochement with the system. A typical example would be Akkie Shonfield – Akkie was short for Akiba – who would become Sir Andrew Shonfield, Director of Chatham House. Akkie had been conventionally progressive, certain that the system could be made over; all that was needed was a new social morality. While he was still up he had registered to do a B.Litt. degree, setting down as the subject of his dissertation, appropriately enough, 'Marx's theory of social morality'. One evening, when he was back on home leave from Alexander's staff, he was with a group of us at a performance of *The Ascent of F6*. We were chatting about the scene in the play in which the climbers inveigh against the use of pitons and other 'artificial' aids by the rival teams attacking the mountain – they were not playing the game. I remarked upon its nostalgia for an age in which you won through by your personal gifts and virtues and commitment alone – the death of the Romantic faith. Akkie said, 'No – it's all about the Oedipus complex!' This view was odd, for though his comment might fit other parts of the play, it was wide of the mark for this one. Akkie was bright but inclined to follow fashion; he was now possessed, like many progressives, by a new, inward-looking philosophy – life was no longer to be explained in terms of 'systems' and boss class manipulation, but by the new Freudian cant. What you must now try to shift was not the world, but *the way you looked at it*. Epitomising this shift, Akkie would come back from the war after distinguished service and become a leader-writer on the *Financial Times*.

Joining the Council kept me in Oxford at a time when I would have preferred to shake its dust off for good. The occupying force, the colonising city of individual and institutional evacuees, began to drift back to London. Occupied colleges would soon reclaim their buildings. The departments of the British Council in Oriel would move out to Blenheim Palace in the wake of the departed intelligence organisation. Here was another unforeseen, unforgettable, dream-like stage on the road from the Gorbals, to walk through the ducal park at lunchtime, look out from my office window over its calm, aristocratic greenery to the John Churchill obelisk, and hear, through the vibrating wall of my room on a gleaming summer afternoon, transcendental Bach on the chapel organ. In this Arcadian quiet of glistening green, profusion of scents, *mise en scène* of baroque opulence and confidence, we were separated by epochal distances from the collapse of worlds. Yet we knew it was all very close, just across the horizon. It was surely wrong to be here? This glittering ambience was too good to last, and rightly so, too insulated, yet spilling over with questioning about the future. Exemplifying the unreality, the detachment, a few yards away down the stately corridor John Betjeman passed the hours chalking intricate notations of change-ringing courses on the plywood wall-coverings!

Soon – it could not be soon enough for me – the Council would home back to London and take me with it. London must be my next citadel.

I would then be married; and realise, after a little time – again too late – the wisdom of John Buyers, my tutor at Glasgow University extension classes, in a letter to me, newly arrived in Oxford: 'many students make the mistake of forming relationships at university on intellectual grounds alone; the necessary emotional substance is often absent . . .' But that is a story for another time.

VE Day would come and go with a huge bonfire at the Martyrs' Memorial, and sudden orgiastic couplings on the pavements in the indifferent night, as a huge crowd seethed in mindless release along the length of the Giler, the contents of the apocalyptic crucible, a boiling mass of lost, directionless bodies, defiant, exulting in forgetful release, with nothing in view, faintly nostalgic for the stilled, provisional life that had been the war, when the future need not be faced.

In the light of the leaping orange flames, with little groups of free-booting foragers breaking through the mass of exulting bodies with freshly purloined fuel – tables from pubs, pieces of fencing, empty barrels, bedsteads – Domenico climbed to the topmost step of the Memorial in his black cloak lined with scarlet, and in the infernal fiery light stretched out his hands, saturnine features livid now, in a hectic but solemn benediction, his sojourn here at last over; then he jumped down and was lost in the crowd. I never saw him again. Whether he regained his unknown homeland I never heard. Over the years, rumours would filter back, attributing to him various avatars – playboy, aristocratic mercenary, professional gambler. He was cast by fortune as a dedicated misfit, though in his fashion made for higher things – in the ranks of the Gentlemen – if the world had not been out of joint. In him was another loser – for no very good reason – saddened at the passing of the only world he could call his own; in comparison with which all else, not meeting his patrician standards, was unworthy.

Still, if Domenico could not realise the aspirations he had inherited, he at least *knew* what they were! What was I left with? If I had been born with any goals, I had no idea what they were – or so I thought. As far as I could see I possessed intellectual equipment but very little else – certainly no conscious compulsion as to where and how to employ it. At my back was a vacuum. Unlike most others here, my background contained nothing that I was driven to preserve. At least I did not then think so. Later I would realise that my passion to shore up crumbling tradition under attack by 'progress', to oppose the shedding of values proven by time, must have begun then, perhaps even earlier, in the Gorbals.

What other assets did I possess? Laski had remarked that I had a talent for scepticism. I could analyse with the rigour of Occam's Razor. Was that what Destiny had in store for me, to stand out against received opinion all my life, and suffer the combined fates of Cassandra and Sisyphus? What a future!

I could make dreams explicit. I would write a novel. It would remain hidden, but parts of its essence would speak again and again in other work. Before I started writing I chose the title – *A Parcel of Their Fortunes*, from *Antony and Cleopatra:*

> 'Men's judgments are
> A parcel of their fortunes, and things outward
> Do draw the inward quality after them,
> To suffer all alike.'

That title, though I did not know it then, would contain the *leitmotiv* of all I would write and do in the future, a consistency of vision I never realised I possessed until now, as I write these words.

The journey from the Gorbals had not ended after all. It would continue at every moment – not always with a backward glance, for in a sense I would, at last, take the place *with me*, with all its ghosts.